MW01122312

Monetising Innovation

Endorsements

Vijay Govindrajan, Leading Global Management Guru, Tuck School of Business and the Marvin Bower Fellow at Harvard

Business scenarios constantly evolve and become more complex and challenging as the years progress. In changing times, Innovation has come to be accepted as a means of enabling businesses to stay ahead of the curve and deliver consistent growth. While the importance of innovation is well known, the challenge lies in translating the Innovation process into a pragmatic and executable market plan. It is at this stage of implementing this thought into practice that most businesses seem to falter.

In '**Monetising Innovation**', the author explains through a well-thought process just how this could be done in a real-life scenario. The suggested framework is flexible and also provides for inputs from all perspectives : the marketplace, customers, internal departments and regulatory compulsions that would enable organisations to cut through the clutter and bring out the key innovation drivers that could be leveraged for profit.

The author has devised a pragmatic framework called ICaM (Innovation Capability Model) that defines drivers that are critical to business organisations. These drivers can guide an organisation in its Innovation capability assessment and steer it in developing pragmatic business plans for the marketplace. The author illustrates the use of this model through powerful case studies from three divergent industries operating out of both, mature and evolving markets.

With Innovate or perish being a reality in most businesses, this model can help organisations to focus on those Innovation drivers that they can truly leverage to grow their market dominance. A separate chapter also delineates on how the results of the Innovation focus and efforts could be measured. The suggested framework is industry-agnostic and can be used in any of the stages of an organisation's life cycle.

The author shows promise in his sound conceptual understanding of Innovation and the practical challenges around its implementation. His work moves beyond these concepts to develop a structural model that could find use in a business environment. In today's competitive space, organisations would find themselves placing increasing reliance on Innovation capability and this book is a welcome narrative that would enable businesses move closer to realising their Innovation potential and truly profiting from it.

Sunil Sood, Managing Director and CEO, Vodafone India
Innovation, driven as a structured process can provide a sustainable competitive edge to an organization. The book *Monetising Innovation* does just that and lays out a pragmatic architecture for driving business Innovation. The structured framework ICaM is an integration of Innovation Drivers across business value chain with focus on delivering superior business results. The framework also draws it's strength from industry agnostic applicability. It is an excellent roadmap to take an organisation to the next level in result oriented Innovation.

Christian D Shaefer, Director, Director Product Development – Financial Services Industry, Frankfurt, Germany
Monetising Innovation is a wonderful book – it offers a holistic overview on the relevant models of innovation and the Innovation Capability Model introduced complements the literature on Innovation. This model enables its corporate user not only to assess the current state of its innovation model but more importantly provides a practical guide for further improvement. The book addresses the needs of anyone in the organization who is concerned with innovation. Its insides are applicable from the working level up to the C-suite. It is fun to read and the cases studies introduced eases the implementation of the ICaM model.

Dr. R K Padhy, Asst. Professor of Operation Management, IIM Kashipur, India
If how to benefit from innovation deployment in Organisation has always baffled you, the book *Monetising Innovation* is the key to unlock the mystery in simple language. The best way to assess and analyse the innovation deployment across organisations has been illustrated in some 200 pages. The three major elements of the book are its simplicity, illustrates the practical insights of application in manufacturing and service organisations and ease of applicability in both Indian and global context. Management students can greatly benefit from the book and can unravel the most frequently used words in today's business called

Innovation. In last few years I have come across very few books like this, which made assessment and application of innovation simple for a practitioner.

Dr. Kirankumar S. Momaya, Professor, Management of Technology/ Innovation and International Competitiveness, Shailesh J. Mehta School of Management, IIT Bombay

This is a useful source for professionals looking for recent views on innovation. A structured framework proposed in the book—ICaM—can help. The book builds on several classical concepts and also gives cases. As large countries such as India attempt basic balances in an "information era', catch-up on different types of innovations, including product and technological, is becoming important. Institutes such as IIT Bombay—with evolving ecosystem of invention, incubation and entrepreneurship—are contributing a lot to innovation. Well planned book with framework and tools for innovators to experiment.

Amit Das, Director- Human Resources, Bennett Coleman & Company Ltd (Times of India group).

Innovation has always been a critical differentiator in providing service, creating a product, or in devising new operational methodology, and continues to be a major contributor to an organisation's success and sustainable growth. In **'Monetising Innovation'**, the author has not only highlighted its significance in the business context, but has also addressed the question of how to measure and effectively leverage Innovation through a systematic framework called ICaM (Innovation Capability Model). The author has illustrated the use of this model across divergent industries, and helped demonstrate the effectiveness through powerful case studies. I'm quite certain that the book will turn out to be a great piece for readers ranging from CXO level executives to Business Managers and Business management students, who can pick up the insights to drive innovation leading to disproportionate enterprise value creation.

Anthony Marsala, Chief Operating Officer, Madison Street Capital, Chicago, US

As a Chief Operating Officer and co-founder of an international boutique investment bank, this book is an extraordinary and invaluable piece on innovation in business. The ICaM framework gives a reader an essential road map on how to utilize an innovation model in a practical way to guide a business from point A to point B, with results. Innovation sometimes is defined as a new way of doing things. This book is innovative in its own right. If you want to read the next disruptive business book on innovation that is easily applicable, **Monetising Innovation** is a must read.

Sanjeev Agarwal, Country Managing Director, Protiviti India

The ever-changing marketplace, technological disruptions, agile competitors and demanding customers and shareholders are only some of the 21st-century realities that are testing organizations around the world. Innovation in the face of these challenges can be a catalyst for growth and success of a business. Gautam Kr Borah's book 'Monetising Innovation sees Innovation through new eyes by putting together a structured approach 'ICaM' for robust implementation. The book goes beyond just defining Innovation and suggests a practical framework to successfully deploy Innovation in business. 'Monetising Innovation' would definitely be of interest to Business professionals, academics and consultants alike as it illustrates the practical applicability of Innovation methods to modern business, with a view to delivering more value sooner and staying ahead in the marketplace.

Purushottam Kaushik, Managing Director, Cisco Systems, India

The book Monetising Innovation addresses a very important challenge of current business environment in almost every sphere whether it is manufacturing, telecom, marketing or government as well. The dynamics in business is changing so fast on account of technology led business models that innovation has become the key for any business. In this background, this book "Monetizing Innovation" from Gautam Borah is an excellent read. Offering a comprehensive overview of Innovation models and also a frame work called ICaM to approach the current business challenges. It not just addresses the view from top executives rather also provides an excellent structure for everyone in business world. Also the language is simple and case studies are very interesting which makes it almost a perfect fun read.

Monetising Innovation

ICaM – A structured framework

GAUTAM KR. BORAH

Foreword by
Dr Marc J Ventresca
Faculty in Strategy and Innovation,
University of Oxford
Co-author of "Routines, 'Going Concerns'
and Innovation"

B L O O M S B U R Y
NEW DELHI • LONDON • OXFORD • NEW YORK • SYDNEY

First published in India 2015

© 2015 by Gautam Kr. Borah

Note: All the introductory quotes before the start of each part are from
Lewis Carroll's *Alice in Wonderland*

ISBN 978 93 848 9835 9
2 4 6 8 10 9 7 5 3 1

Bloomsbury Publishing India Pvt. Ltd
DDA Complex, LSC Building No.4
Second Floor, Pocket C – 6 & 7, Vasant Kunj
New Delhi 110070
www.bloomsbury.com

Typeset by Manmohan Kumar
Printed and bound in India by Gopsons Papers Ltd

To find out more about our authors and books visit www.bloomsbury.com.
Here you will find extracts, author interviews, details of forthcoming
events and the option to sign up for our newsletters.

To my family
for
being with me every moment

Contents

PART 4: STRUCTURE OF BUSINESS INNOVATION — ICaM

PART 5: CASE CONTEXTS — APPLICATION OF ICAM IN XMOBILE, ALLHEALTHCARE, AND SMITHHAN TOOLS

PART 6: ASSESSMENT AND ANALYSIS

PART 7: CONCLUSION

List of Figures

List of Tables

Foreword

Here is a book that combines thoughtful integration of current research, with detailed and extensive interviews with practitioners, along with the author's eye to notice what can accelerate innovation impact.

This is a timely book, motivated by one of the critical challenges facing businesses today: How to innovate in regular, reliable ways? In *Monetising Innovation*, Gautam Borah presents the distilled insights of research, reading, and practical experience to focus on innovation that connects early capacity steps with implementation and innovation results. The focus is on identifying and specifying organizational and leadership levers for innovation impact. The purpose is to present innovation as a core organizational function and to describe the shift from occasional and *ad hoc* innovation to reliable, routine innovation.

The book develops recent research findings that explore innovation as a corporate function that can be designed, staffed and resourced to grow both capacity and experience for successful innovation. Borah starts from core premises in the technology strategy and innovation literature: That an 'innovation system' in organizational terms distinguishes 'invention' from the development activities needed to generate 'innovation' and further distinguishes 'innovation' from technology transfer and from commercialization, growth, and business results (Hughes 1983). The value of this careful set of distinctions leads directly to practical insights about how best to structure and resource purposeful innovation initiatives. (Hargadon 2003; Pisano 2015).

The guiding premise here is that sustained, regular innovation is critical for long-term business success and, more basically, continued viability in the kind of turbulent, complex business contexts that characterize industries and markets today (Ventresca and Kaghan 2008). And that said innovation isn't the accumulation of chance, or the work of a few brilliant employees, or simply a function of resource abundance. Instead, the research argument and evidence focuses on the design and implementation of a purposeful innovation 'value chain' (Hansen and Birkinshaw 2007) with supporting process, talent, and senior leadership attention.

The book introduces the Innovation Capability Model (ICaM), an integrated framework that connects findings from research on effective innovation systems. The Framework incorporates 18 critical drivers that connect initial intent with effective implementation and innovation results. The Framework features five clusters of implementation drivers: Assessment of Innovation Trend, Innovation Strategy and Leadership Support, Resource Management for Innovation, Innovation Process, and Innovation Results.

'Innovation' is a common focus in many business conversations and contexts today. Too often, though 'innovation' takes form in aspirational conversations that want for application, or in too situated a setting, that wants for broader impact. Or, also too frequently, firms reserve the word 'innovation' for technology changes that extend current markets and technologies with attention to many others sites for innovation that can directly improve performance today and over time. The strengths of this book are several. They address and extend such analysis:

- Research-based findings: The book is research-based. The author has done extensive secondary research and interviewed practitioners and professionals to arrive at initial findings. These findings have been tested in a few organizations, these cases used to refine and focus the patterns of initial results.
- Quantified Measurement: The ICaM framework assigns numeric weights to each driver thus creating a tool to assess and act on areas for needed focus, improvements, and sustained attention.

- Outcome-focused: The ICaM framework focuses intensely on business results from innovation
- Case Studies: The research findings are illustrated with selected case studies, to foster the reinforce the lessons of actual business situations and to support real life scenarios
- Supporting Content: The content, specifically the Innovation Primer around the core model of ICaM, provides a crisp and sharp analysis on various perspectives on Innovation

I first worked with Gautam Borah in the strategy and innovation course at Said Business School. In those earliest meetings, his structured curiosity about how innovation works and how firms can promote and measure innovation more effectively was vivid. This book is a developed outcome of that sustained curiosity. This work is a singular accomplishment of an experienced practitioner, who invested time and effort to read, integrate, and formulate an actionable to reliable innovation.

Marc J Ventresca, Faculty in Strategy and Innovation
University of Oxford
Co-author of "Routines, 'Going Concerns' and Innovation"
Oxford, UK
2015

References

Hansen, M.T. 2007. "The Innovation Value Chain." Harvard Business Review, June 85(6): 121-131.

Hargardon, A. 2003. *How Breakthroughs Happen: The Surprising Truth About How Companies Innovate*. Harvard Business School Press.

Hughes, T.P. 1983/1993. *Networks of Power: Electrification in Western Society 1880-1930*. Johns Hopkins University Press.

Pisano, G.P. 2015. "You Need An Innovation Strategy." *Harvard Business Review*, June pp 44-54.

Ventresca, M.J. and W.N. Kaghan. 2008. "Routines, 'Going Concerns' and Innovation: Towards an Evolutionary Economic Sociology." Chapter 4 in M.C. Becker (ed.), *Handbook of Organizational Routines*. Edward Elgar Publishing.

PART 1

Introduction

'Begin at the beginning', the King said, very gravely,
'And
go on till you come to the end: then stop.'

CHAPTER 1

Why another book on Innovation?

The book ... in just a minute ...

This book presents a pragmatic framework called **ICaM (Innovation Capability Model)** that comprises innovation drivers critical to business organisations.

The work is based on the research by the author as part of the Post Graduate Programme in Strategy and Innovation from the University of Oxford (2013). The framework was further developed through advanced industry and relevant research, and applied with success in a few firms across the manufacturing and service sectors.

The framework was presented by the author at the *6th Annual Conference for Oxford Academy of Innovation and Entrepreneurship (August, 2013)* and was acclaimed by the fraternity.

Why another book on Innovation?

Companies from various sectors were studied, as well as views of industry leaders were analysed to understand the industry context of innovation. The industry context analysis reveals a chasm experienced by business organisations, while assessing innovation capability. Organisations, as revealed during the analysis, embark on a journey of innovation, with various objectives ranging from sustaining growth, achieving cost leadership, or to adapt and diversify in a defined market. However, discussions with the senior management as well as innovation practitioners evinced the lack of a common, trusted, and tested framework to assess where a firm stands in the journey of innovation.

This is a precarious situation resembling when one embarks on a long sailing without a compass, reaches the mid sea, and become clueless about the direction. As evinced during the study, business organisations leverage on innovation to achieve various organisational goals. However, due to lack of a proper framework, very often, the efforts tend to lose steam midway.

It is thus perceived as a dire need to have a tested and trusted framework, which can act as a guide in an innovation journey of a business firm.

This book fills the gap

This book is an effort to fill this void. Organisations can use the ICaM framework to assess the current level of the innovation capability. Also, ICaM can be adopted to decide on the innovation drivers to focus, thus enabling a firm to navigate in the right direction with the optimum use of resources.

The research and the book are based on strong fundamental sources of inputs, such as organizational study, literature research, case studies, and expert discussions. The ICaM Framework has been developed predicated on the inputs, and it comprises 18 innovation drivers, with numerical significance assigned to each. The framework was comprehensively applied in few business organisations from sectors as TMT (Telecom/ Media/Technology), manufacturing, and services. The results were validated with success, and the framework has been recommended for adoption in organisations setting out on an innovation journey.

CHAPTER 2

Who should use this book?

'*We cannot solve a problem by using the same kind of thinking we used when we created them.*'

This quote from Albert Einstein probably posits the inherent rationale of the book. It provides a framework to first baseline an organisation in an innovation campaign, and to further steer it in the right direction with optimum resources. In the context of usage, the book views the users from two perspectives – *individual users and business organisations*.

Individual Users

CXOs

CXOs can use the book to create the Innovation blueprint for the organisation. This comprises creation of baseline, defining the innovation strategy, provision of resources, and ensuring business benefits.

Innovation Leads

Innovation leads can use this book as a step-by-step guide to drive innovation. This can be further used for measuring the current levels of innovation, and hence identification of the areas to focus.

Business Managers

Business managers can use the relevant part of the framework to drive innovation in the respective functional areas.

Consultants

The book can act as a guide to consultants in helping an organisation to drive innovation. This subsumes creation of baseline, as well as driving innovation customised to the specific organisation.

Students (Business Management)

The short primer section in the book can be a guide to comprehend innovation from various dimensions. Further, ICaM framework can augment the understanding of the innovation maxims from the perspective of application beyond a notional level.

Business Organisations

The background research included samples from a wide spectrum of industries and respondents. The framework was further tested in business organisations from various sectors. This has rendered the framework industry-agnostic to a substantiative degree. However, there may be exceptions and deviations entailing customisation, which are discussed in the relevant sections.

CHAPTER 3

Structure and how to use the book

Figure 3.1 illustrates the structure of the book

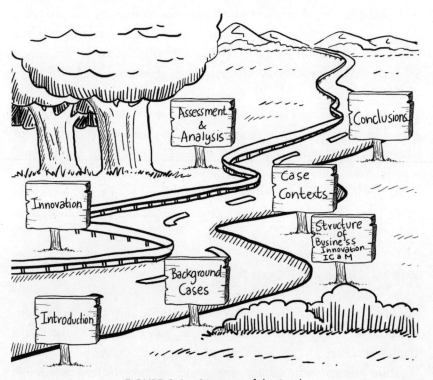

FIGURE 3.1   Structure of the Book

The core of the book is ICaM, and the rest of the chapters are built around the core. Readers are expected to reach the core of the book by a step-by-step approach.

Part 1: Introduction

Introduction portrays a generic background to the book and comprises four chapters. First chapter presents the background and rationale of the book. While the second chapter delineates the user domain, the current chapter (chapter3) is an explication of the book structure, to enable readers to navigate with efficacy. Chapter four is an illustration of expected business benefits that a firm can expect from using the book.

Part 2: Background Cases

The objective of this part is to impart a real life flavour to the application of ICaM framework in an organisation, and comprises five chapters. Three cases from different sectors have been illustrated from the imaginary country of Athena. The first case is of XMobile, the largest telecom service provider in Athena. The biggest integrated healthcare firm in Athena, AllHealthCare, represents the second case being espoused for discussion. SmithHan Tools, based in Athena, is the largest global player in hand tools, which represents the third case picked up for analysis. Organisations have been selected from various sectors, and represent the characteristics of archetypal situations organisations face, while driving innovation. These cases have been frequently referred to in the later sections for illustrating the concepts and the framework in real-life scenarios.

Part 3: Innovation – A Short Primer

For a better understanding, readers are expected to keep abreast of various perspectives of innovation, before delving into the realm of the ICaM framework. Part 3 of the book is predicated on this very apriorism, and is a short primer on the subject. The primer will take the readers through various perspectives of innovation such as definitions of it, S-Curve for predicting technology obsolescence, innovation ecosystem, role of people in driving innovation, maxims of open innovation, measuring innovation capability, etc. Besides, innovation paradigms practiced in Apple, 3M and Google have been analysed in detail. While Part 3 can be used by innovation practitioners to inspirit the current knowledge base, readers new to the subject can leverage it to comprehend the building blocks of innovation. This part adverts to cases in Part 2. in exemplifying the concepts.

Part 4: Structure of Business Innovation – ICaM

Part 4 is the kernel of the book. This section explains various drivers and requirements of innovation in a business firm. Five components of ICaM (referred to as Clusters) namely *Assessment of Innovation Trends*, *Innovation Strategy and Leadership Support*, *Resource Management for Innovation*, *Innovation Process*, and *Innovation Results* are presented in this section, along with elaborative detail of the 18 innovation drivers that comprise the Clusters.

Part 5: Case Contexts – Application of ICaM in XMobile, AllHealthCare, and SmithHan Tools

Part 5 extends the framework to the application level and illustrates the use of ICaM framework, citing the cases as examples. Cases of XMobile, AllHealthCare, and SmithHan Tools exemplify how an organisation deploys the 18 innovation drivers (as explained in part 4) in a structured manner.

Part 6: Assessment and Analysis

An explanation of how ICaM can be deployed and innovation performance assessed constitutes the essence of Part 6. This part contains four chapters. The first chapter (Chapter 22) is an explanation of the fundamentals to deploy ICaM in an organisation. The next chapter

(Chapter 23) illustrates how to assess innovation performance and create a baseline for future reference. Chapter 24 is about expressing innovation performance and ferrets out various measures and metrics to indicate achievement. The last chapter (Chapter 25) is an account of illustrative results, taking the reference of XMobile.

Part 7: Conclusion

This part is a sketch for senior management. First chapter named *Recipe for the CEO* reinforces how a structured framework like ICaM can be used by an organisation to stay competitive through sustained and result-oriented innovation.

Recommendations, the last chapter of the book, explicate the recommendation for use of ICaM, level of perfection of the framework, as well as the art and science of deploying it in an organisation.

Appendices

Appendix I is the ICaM instrument, derived from the ICaM framework, which is the base for assessment of innovation capability of an organisation.

Appendix II contains discussion questions from the relevant chapters.

CHAPTER 4

Business Benefits

This book primarily approaches innovation from the perspective of *application,* with business results from innovation as the focal point. At the same time, elements of innovation theories have been discussed in the appropriate places for a student to comprehend innovation across the spectrum from concept to application. Especially, the discussion questions in the appendix can be used by students to build concepts, and further extend to application.

With the use of the book, business organisations are expected to accrue benefits from the following perspectives.

Improvement in top line and bottom line

The book views innovation *as 'Innovation = Invention + Commercialisation + Business Benefits'* (Chapter 10: Innovation – A Short Primer) and the framework has a clear emphasis on business results (weight of 40 per cent: Chapter 11 – Structure of ICaM). The innovation results are linked with top line or bottom line benefits, like penetration in the desired market, sales from the commercialised ideas, EBIT from the commercialised ideas, or the time to break even. Thus, an organisation adopting the framework can expect to behold an improvement in top line or bottom line or both.

Creating a Continuous stream of innovation

One of the most critical components of the framework is an end-to-end process from idea generation to conversion to products, till commercialisation of the profitable ideas (Chapter 11 – Structure of ICaM). The framework accentuates open sources of idea sourcing, besides the traditional approach of internal sources. This balanced focus is expected to provide an edge to an organisation deploying the ICaM framework in the context of a continuous flow of ideas, to convert to profitable product streams.

Helping to build a culture of innovation

Albeit business result being the focal point, the framework provides a holistic leeway, encompassing market process and people linked to business results in a structured manner. It would be a balanced surmise that an organisation adopting the framework can expect to build a culture of innovation over a defined period of time.

PART 2

Background Cases

'Alice: Would you tell me, please, which way I ought to go from here?
The Cheshire Cat: That depends a good deal on where you want to get to.
Alice: I don't much care where.
The Cheshire Cat: Then it doesn't much matter which way you go.
Alice: ... So long as I get somewhere.
The Cheshire Cat: Oh, you're sure to do that, if only you walk long enough.'

CHAPTER 5

Background Cases – A Brief

Concepts and theories entail a linkage with real life applications. In this context, the book has integrated the concepts and the framework with real life case studies.

This book refers to three firms as cases, while discussing the concepts and the ICaM framework.

The firms being discussed belong to an imaginary country, Athena. However, there is less imagination and fantasy, and there is a balanced dose of reality – multiple reviews, analyses, and iterations have been carried out, so that the country and the cases reflect real life scenarios, easier for the readers to connect.

While the cases have been elaborated in the subsequent sections with detailed analysis, the brief below is an account for a quick browse.

Country of Athena

The country of Athena, known as Federal Republic of Athena, is located in the Southern hemisphere with a population of more than 230 million. It is a country with rich cultural heritage, and became independent from colonial rule in 1954. Currently, it is a democratic republic with 13 states. All the firms whose cases are referred have strong operating bases in Athena.

Case 1: XMobile

XMobile is the largest telecom service provider in Athena, across all 13 states, with more than 70 million subscribers. The current Revenue Market Share (RMS) of XMobile is more than 36 per cent.

Case 2: AllHealthCare

AllHealthCare is the largest integrated healthcare firm in Athena. Part of a global group, the healthcare giant entered into an agreement with the Government of Athena in the year 1970, and currently provides its services across basic care, special care, and super specialty care, mostly focussing on cities and small towns

Case 3: SmithHan Tools

SmithHan Tools is one of the top global hand tool manufacturers present in Athena. With the largest base in the country, SmithHan operates in nine countries, with more than 35 per cent global market share. Currently, SmithHan Tools is contemplating the idea to diversify in the domain of machine tools.

CHAPTER 6

Federal Republic of Athena

Athena — A Mystical Past

The great country of Athena is located in the southern hemisphere, near the islands of Dione. The three-sided land-locked nation has the sea on its western and southern regions. Originally called Athenela, the country of Athena has a rich history of over 3000 years. The story of Neladmitri – an ancient emperor of the land of Athena, has been immortalised in the Athenian epic 'Granthnela'. If age-old scriptures are to be believed, Neladmitri conquered the original Athenela, and ruled the land in peace and harmony. The subjects of the land were so happy with their able king, that they blessed him and prayed that his name lives on forever; and that's how the name 'Athenela' came into being.

Athena is one of the oldest inhabited regions on the planet. The Aurora Valley Civilization, which spread and flourished in the northwestern part of Athena, was the first major civilization in the southern hemisphere. Archaeological excavations of the area suggest an extremely early date for human habitation and technology in the area. The areas of present-day Athena have provided archaeologists and scholars with the richest sites in the world. The excavations in the past hundred years have dramatically changed the understanding of Athena's ancient times. The people of the

FIGURE 6.1   Map of Athena

Aurora Valley Civilization worshipped many gods, and engaged in ritual worship. They were nature worshippers as well.

Athena was subject to various foreign influences and powers, until finally gaining its independence in 1954.

The current map of Athena is as in the Figure 6.1.

Athena Today

The country now has 13 states and a population of about 230 million. With a tropical climate, the country is dependent largely on the monsoons in many parts. Although Athena primarily used to be an agrarian country, in the last 10 years, the booming young population has largely shifted its focus to the manufacturing and service sector.

Athena's literacy rate is 93.5 per cent, and this makes her one of the highly literate countries in the world. The country has a multi-cultural and a multi-lingual set up, with each state having its own language. Although there are many languages and dialects spoken in Athena, Neliya can be considered a language spoken commonly in most parts of the country. The English language is used by the country's urban population, and is considered as the common language for business and networking. The country's currency is Athenian Dollar, and currently, 25 Athenian Dollars is equivalent to a US Dollar.

Political Athena

The government of Athena is a federal republic, set up by a constitution adopted in 1960. The two houses of the Athenian regime are alluded as the upper and lower house. The lower house representatives are elected by the people, while the upper house representatives are nominated by the lower house, as well as the state assemblies. The president is the constitutional head, and is elected by the people. There are two prominent political parties – Peoples Progressive Party (PPP) and Republican Congress Party (RCP). PPP believes in a reformative approach and RCP is regarded as a party with a conservative outlook. PPP has been in power for the last 10 years.

Demographic Indicators

The following table (Table 6.1) is an illustration of current demographic indicators of Athena. A large percentage of its population (61.81%) lives in the rural hinterlands, while the remaining (38.79%) makes up for the urban populace. With Athena's continuous focus on health and safety, the life expectancy has improved to 75 years in the last 10 years,

TABLE 6.1   Athena Demographic Indicators

Population (Mn)	230.0 (38.79% Urban and 61.81% Rural)
Population Growth Rate	0.03%
Life Expectancy	75 Years
Sex Ratio	980 Females to 1000 Males

as compared to the earlier 60. Presently, population growth rate is 0.03 per cent, with sex ratio at 980 females for every 1000 males.

Population Distribution

The population distribution of Athena in terms of geography is shown in the following diagram (Figure 6.2).

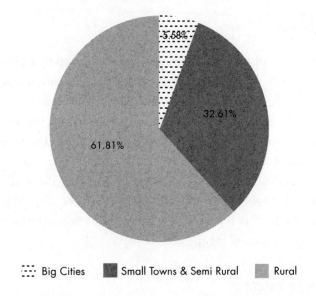

:::: Big Cities   ▓ Small Towns & Semi Rural   ▓ Rural

FIGURE 6.2   Population distribution of Athena

The entities have been defined as per the following guidelines set by the Government of Athena, Department of Statistics.

Big Cities
- Population above 0.5 million
- More than 70 per cent of people are engaged in non-agrarian activities

Small Towns and Semi-Rural
- Minimum population of 5000
- Have a town board or committee
- More than 50 per cent of people are engaged in non-agrarian activities

Rural
- Comprises villages or block of villages
- More than 50 per cent of people are engaged in agriculture or other farming activities

One of the biggest boons for Athena's growth is her very young population (Figure 6.3).

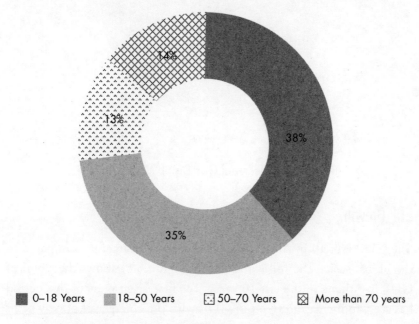

| ■ 0–18 Years | 18–50 Years | 50–70 Years | More than 70 years |

FIGURE 6.3   Age-wise population distribution of Athena

The median age group is 25.2 years. 38 per cent of the population is below 18 years.

Current Economic Scenario

The current GDP of Athena is in the tune of US $ 1200 billion. The highest contribution to Athena's GDP is the service sector (48 per cent), followed by manufacturing (35 per cent), and then agriculture (17 per cent). However, agriculture sector is perpetually marked by low productivity, with more than 45 per cent people engaged in it. Figure 6.4 is a representation of the sectorial GDP distribution.

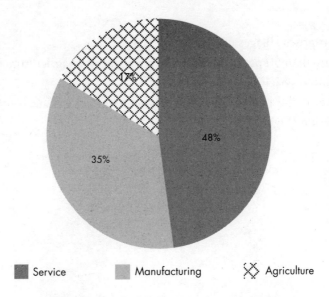

FIGURE 6.4   Sectorial GDP Distribution of Athena

GDP Growth

The GDP growth in Athena has been quite encouraging, compared to the global scale. The following figure (Figure 6.5) shows the trend of GDP in Athena in the last 10 years. The first seven years of this period has seen an increasing trend in GDP, with the emergence of new firms in the service sector, with a global presence. However, the last three years have been disappointing with a dwindling trend. Though experts'

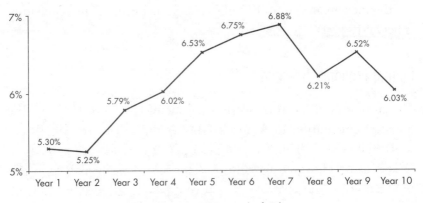

FIGURE 6.5   GDP trend of Athena

projection indicated a GDP greater than 8 per cent in the current year, it has come down to hover around just above 6 per cent.

However, global rating agencies view this as a short-term hiccup, rather than a harbinger of a slow growth. Their confidence has been boosted by the rich natural resources of the country, large young population, emergence of considerable number of firms with global presence, as well as a progressive outlook of the current regime.

The government has taken cognizance of the fact, and Robert Mucci, Athena's Industry Minister, recently stated in an interview with the Athenian press, 'The need of the hour is to focus on the fundamentals. Service sector alone can't help Athena grow. We have to pull up our socks and focus on other core sectors too. One of the major areas where our attention has to be diverted towards is agricultural productivity. We seem to have forgotten our agrarian past. At the same time, we need to rejuvenate the manufacturing sector to at least double the GDP contribution. Innovation will be a key differentiator for us. There is so much we can do; we need to innovate in the right direction and right spirit.'

Background Case 1 – XMobile

Thud! And the door closes. Claire realised that probably for Hugh, the board meeting didn't go as planned. She quietly tip-toed to his cabin door and knocked but there was not that usual warm response. She slowly opened the door to find Hugh sitting at his desk with a look of worry written all across his face. She knew something had to go really wrong for the cool, composed, and usually the calm demeanor, seemed to have vanished.

'Hugh seemed to be in a state of reverie.' Claire thought. She was curious what might have transpired in the board meeting.

Hugh is the managing director of XMobile, the biggest telecom operator in Athena, and Claire is his deputy – the chief executive officer, looking after XMobile operations across the country. This is Hugh's third year in the company. He took over the reign of XMobile at a troubled time, and could pull up the performance of the company with focus on execution and cost effectiveness, stressing more on the bottom line. During his tenure, the numbers rallied substantially – the Revenue Market Share (RMS) improved from about 30 per cent to more than 36 per cent and EBITDA (Earing Before Interest Tax, Depreciation, and Amortisation) improved from 22 per cent to more than 28 per cent.

However, there has been disturbing news around in the last two years with AirNet, the second largest operator catching up on all fronts, and as expected, today's board meeting was not a cake walk for Hugh. There were questions on the current strategy of focussing on the bottom line, and there were more queries on the way forward, and why XMobile could not create an upsurge by venturing into new areas to inflate the top line too.

'The situation is becoming flinty day by day.', Hugh pondered with a deep sigh….

Claire's voice suddenly brought him back from his reverie, to find his right hand person staring at him intently. 'I am sorry Claire; I didn't realise you were around. There are even more reasons to worry than the surge of AirNet. Though in the initial stage, the news of SkyFone taking 25 per cent of AirNet's stake has been confirmed to be true. They are global leaders in data services and product innovations.'

Hugh continued, 'It definitely seems like a bumpy road ahead.'

Claire knew Hugh was right in his assessment – another front had opened after today's board meeting!!

XMobile – A journey of 12 years

XMobile started its operations 12 years ago as a paging company in two states of Athena, when paging was the state-of-the-art technology. Over these years, XMobile has grown in leaps and bounds to become the number one telecom company in Athena. Industry analysts have marked three distinct phases of growth for XMobile:

- **Footprint** – *In the first five years, XMobile was focussed on customer acquisition and on gross addition of subscribers, with clear focus on topline growth.*
- **Consolidation** – *The second phase lasted nearly five years and has seen XMobile creating markets in other states of Athena. During this time, other telecom businesses were acquired, and Third Generation Network was rolled out.*
- **Controlling** – *The current phase is, where the company has been trying to achieve a controlling market share in all the states. Another strategy of XMobile in this phase is the introduction of breakthrough products and the roll-out of Fourth Generation Network.*

Organisation set-up

XMobile's organisational set up is a functional multi-geography matrix structure (Figure 7.1)

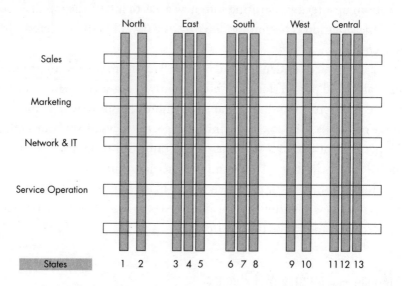

FIGURE 7.1   Organisational structure of XMobile

The operation is organised in five geographies vertically: North, South, East, West, and Central. Each state is a separate business unit headed by a CEO. The state CEOs report to Regional CEOs, who in turn report to the Chief Operating Officer. The horizontal organisation is in line with traditional functions – sales, marketing, service, commercial, hr and finance. XMobile doesn't have a separate product development function. Currently, product development is the responsibility of relevant functional teams such as the marketing and customer service operations.

Market Share

XMobile has a subscriber base of more than 70 million. The current Revenue Market Share is 36.58 per cent (Figure 7.2) and is the highest amongst the telecom operators.

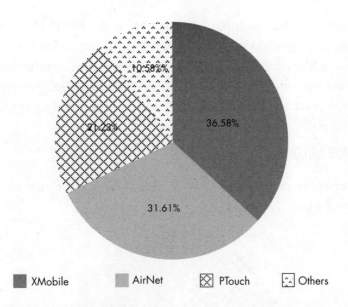

FIGURE 7.2   Revenue Market Share of various telecom service providers

Airnet, the second largest player, trails Xmobile with a share of 31.61 per cent, and PTouch, a third player, contributes a share of 21.23 per cent.

EBITDA Trend

XMobile has a healthy EBITDA trend all across the last four years (Figure 7.3). However, of late, XMobile has been haunted by the nearest

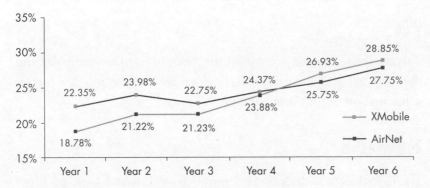

FIGURE 7.3   EBITDA trend of XMobile and the nearest competitor

competitor AirNet, as it has exceeded XMobile's EBITDA margin in the last two years. More worrying has been the fact that it has been sustaining a northward trend. XMobile is assaying to counter this with new customer-focussed initiatives and cost containment. However, the outcome is yet to be evident on the balance sheet to feel soothed.

Revenue Streams

The current revenue streams of XMobile consist of three main channels (Figure 7.4).

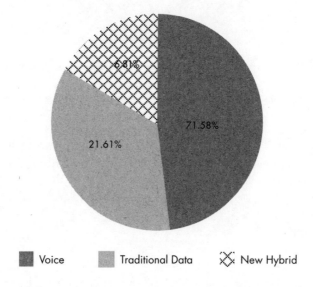

FIGURE 7.4   XMobile product-wise revenue distribution

Voice

This comprises various voice products, both in contract (postpaid) and non-contract (prepaid) categories. Products are designed based on further segmentation of the customer base.

Traditional Data

Traditional data includes text messaging services and basic packages for internet.

New Hybrid

This is a new product category launched by XMobile just about a year ago. The new hybrid products are mostly sector-specific data products with substantial share by apps (applications).

XMobile mostly depends on traditional voice revenue, which is about 71.58 per cent of the total service revenue (Figure 7.4). While new hybrid products are gaining momentum due to a continuous focus, coupled with a distinct pull from the market, traditional data products still contribute a substantial share.

Geographical revenue break-up

Compared in a geographic scale, XMobile revenue chest is mostly enriched by the small towns and the semi-rural locations, with about 61.61 per cent share (Figure 7.5). With less focus till recently, rural geography contributes just a meagre 16.81 per cent.

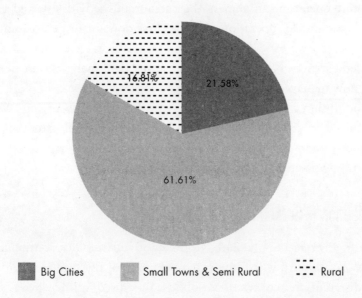

FIGURE 7.5   XMobile geography-wise revenue distribution

The following table (Table 7.1) is a representation of penetration of the products across geographies.

TABLE 7.1   XMobile penetration – product and geography wise

	Voice	Traditional Data	New Hybrid	Overall
Rural	60%	30%	10%	48%
Small Town and Semi Rural	80%	70%	28%	77%
Big Cities	150%	100%	80%	130%

* Figures in weighted average.

On an overall scale, the rural penetration is just above 48 per cent, and insinuates a potential for rapid growth. Penetration in big cities is more than 130 per cent and for the small towns and semi-rural, the figure is nearly 77 per cent, still offering scope for growth.

Outsourcing as a Growth Strategy

XMobile, to deal with the scale and growth, decided to outsource the non-core operations in phases. The outsourcing activities started a few years ago, and IT operations was the first domain to be outsourced. In the next few years, call centers and back offices were outsourced to selected partners. Network maintenance and data analytics were next in line, now managed by globally acknowledged partners.

The upshot of the initiative was typical of any outsourcing. While it resulted in reduction of overheads to a substantial extent, it has given respite to the organisation to channelise its resources to attain a controlling position in the market.

Distribution – Backbone of XMobile

Akin to any telecom operator, XMobile too nurtures distribution as its backbone, around which the core operations of the firm is organised. The distribution network of XMobile is organised in three layers:

XShoppe

These are company-owned outlets, fully maintained by the company.

Retail Outlets

These are any outlet, shop, or establishment, which sell XMobile products. A number of retailers are mapped to one distributor.

Collaborative Retailing

XMobile has also collaborated with the top two multi-brand retailers in the country, who sell XMobile products exclusively at their outlets. This comprises traditional retailing as well as e-tailing by the use of e-commerce platforms.

All the layers are governed by different business models.

Next phase of growth

XMobile is at a crossroad. Currently, traditional voice products contribute the highest revenue share, but are fast approaching the brink of market penetration across geographies. On the other side of the spectrum are the new hybrid products, with a substantial market pull, entailing a continuous stream of market relevant products.

Quoting Hugh, 'We need to be market ready before time. Sustenance of the traditional voice market is the key to survival. But how well we innovate our new hybrid products will define our future. The code of success is a strategic balance of innovation with execution.'

CHAPTER 8

Case 2 – AllHealthCare

1954 – 64: The 'Decade of Death' in Athena

Although Athena can boast of a rich history in most aspects, the legacy of the colonial rule left its health infrastructure in shambles for almost 10 years after its independence. With just the basics in place, that too only in the big city medical centres, the remote areas were entirely dependent on traditional ways of healing, involving unproven herbal medicines, quacks, and even black magic.

Due to its poor medical condition, large population, and low health awareness, Athena as a country experienced a number of epidemics and diseases, especially in the hinterlands in the 50's and 60's. This trend

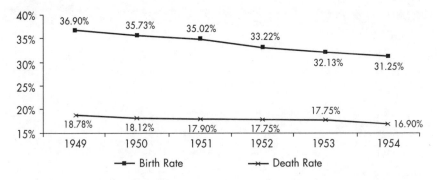

FIGURE 8.1   Athena's birth and death rate

resulted in a high death rate in the country. The above figure (Figure 8.1) indicates the declining trend of Athena's medical history towards its independence, with regards to its birth and death rate.

Contrary to Athena's rich history, which only blossomed further, many health indicators (Table 8.1) proved that its medical journey was on a decline in the 50's.

TABLE 8.1   Athena's health indicators

Life Expectancy at Birth M/F	54/51
Total Expenditure on Health Per capita (In US $)	$ 85
Total Expenditure on Health as % of GDP	1.2%

If this trend continued, Athena's existence was in jeopardy. Considering that not even the basics were in place, Athena had a real challenge on her hands during this period. Something had to be done real soon to get the country back on a healthy track.

1965: The Watershed Year

A defining moment came in the year 1965, which proved to be Athena's path to redemption. The Athenian government came out with the new health policy and charter. The charter stated that health is a basic right for all individuals. Corporates were incentivised to be part of this journey. While the domestic players were encouraged with various incentives, FDI (Foreign Direct Investment) was allowed up to 49 per cent. Athena also had medical centres with basic health planned in each district.

The charter addressed healthcare needs in three layers:
• **Bottom layer** – The basic care with facilities and provision for assessing basic health parameters, as basic blood tests, etc. Graduates and trained medical practitioners, who are not necessarily graduate doctors, were expected to handle these units. These are outpatient facilities available to all. The target was mostly the rural population. The healthcare policy planned to target the one basic care facility for every 100 rural villages.

- **Mid layer** – This represents the specialty care unit. The mid layer units have inpatient facilities and trained doctors with post graduate qualifications and fully equipped lab facilities to handle this unit. This was planned in each district headquarter.
- **Top layer** – The most advanced super specialty unit was to be set up with all facilities and experienced specialists. Research was one of the prime focus of this layer. The charter suggested setting up at least two such units in the first three years.

AllHealthCare – A tryst made with Athena

AllHealthCare is a global name in healthcare, and is a health conglomerate with services across all the verticals of healthcare. It operates in 15 countries, and has been the pioneer in a few path-breaking research innovations.

It entered into an agreement with the Government of Athena in the year 1970 to focus mainly on specialty care and super specialty segments. While it was not a focus, AllHealthcare was also committed to support the government in basic care as well.

Geographic Presence

Current business break-up of AllHealthCare business, according to geographical pattern, is as depicted in the figure below (Figure 8.2). In the current revenue break-up, small towns and semi-rural contribute the maximum, with about 45.63 per cent of market share. Big cities account for about 41.58 per cent of the total share, and rural contributes a meagre 12.79 per cent.

In Its 40 years of existence in Athena, AllHealthCare established about 25 specialty and super-special care units. Two research facilities were also exclusively set up in collaboration with the government. Currently, AllHealthCare is the biggest integrated healthcare player in Athena. However, all these years, rural has never been a focus for AllHealthCare, and its presence in rural areas is limited to training the rural health practitioners.

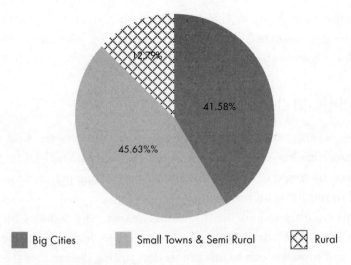

Big Cities	Small Towns & Semi Rural	Rural

FIGURE 8.2   AllHealthCare geography-wise revenue distribution

Current Line of Services and Revenue

Current line of business of AllHealthCare comprises four verticals – *In-patient Care, Out-patient Care, Laboratory, and Research*. In-patient and out-patient services are present in both, bottom and the top layers across geographies. Research is focussed mostly on advanced medical care.

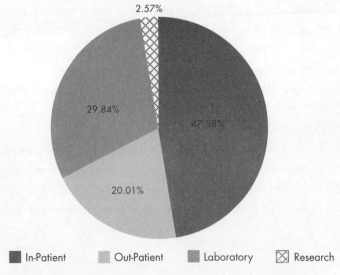

In-Patient	Out-Patient	Laboratory	Research

FIGURE 8.3   AllHealthCare service-wise revenue distribution

As shown in the figure (Figure 8.3), the In-patient care is the biggest revenue generator (47.58 per cent), followed by laboratory services, which contribute about 29.84 per cent.

Current Charter and Road Ahead

The government has recently refreshed the old charter, and rural healthcare has been put in the list of priority sectors. The FDI for rural has been increased to 75 per cent and all the existing players have been asked to put focus on this sector.

This entails a re-look at AllHealthCare's strategy to focus only on urban areas. The firm, in this case, may need to deviate from the core areas, and work towards healthcare services suiting the needs of the rural populace. Currently, like many other healthcare providers in Athena, AllHealthCare doesn't have experience in the rural sector.

In the perspective of the new rural focus, this has posed as a tricky scenario for the management of AllHealthCare. It is a catch-20 situation. While this provides an opportunity to address the needs of a large universe, the expected returns would be meagre.

The challenge faced by the management is to come out with a strategy that relies on innovation, exploit its core competence of research and special healthcare, and at the same time, addresses the need of the rural sector. Blueprint of AllHealthCare outlines the following guiding principles for future:

- *Leverage on innovation as the growth engine*
- *Consolidate urban healthcare by efficiency improvement and capacity utilisation*
- *Rural healthcare as the focus area*

This, stated in the words of AllHealthcare's CEO, 'We need to bank on the past, but explore the future radically. This entails innovation as the growth lever, where we exploit our core competency of urban healthcare, as well as develop and nurture competence to cater to the need of the rural mass.'

CHAPTER 9

Background Case 3 – SmithHan Tools

'It is time I retire; it is time to handover the reigns to Betty, but why am I uncomfortable accepting all the grand plans she has for the company? Why do I feel she is moving too fast and in the wrong direction? Are we really ready for this change?' Ronald Smith turned around in his chair and was now facing the sea from his office window. Deep in thought, he was in his swanky office on the 32nd floor, in one of the buildings in a posh location, overlooking the sea with the full view.

The small sleek phone on the desk suddenly broke the eerie silence with the ring of a bird. He picked up the phone when the chairman's voice flew from the other end, 'Hello Ronald, are you on the report that was discussed today? You think we could agree with what Betty and her young team suggested ?'

'Yes I am thinking about it', Ronald replied. 'I will be ready with an answer before the board meeting next week....'

Ronald Smith, the high profile CEO of SmithHan Tools, a company that was set up by his great grandfather, has witnessed a lot of changes lately due to the emerging market conditions. His daughter Betty, the heiress to this company, has been actively coming up with innovative ideas, and has been constantly telling her father how a change is necessary for SmithHan, not to just survive, but to grow further.

Betty is a go-getter, and her mantra for everything was, 'Go for the kill!' Success was a habit for her. Like her, the report she and the top consulting firm suggested seemed a bit too futuristic for SmithHan Tools.

Their suggestion is to slow down the most profitable line of business (hand tool) and divert to machine tools, which is a big shift for the company. This presentation was discussed that morning with the shareholders, and has been the cause for Ronald's current predicament.

The board was specific in reaction, 'Are we now ready for the new challenge?' It was looking at Ronald for an answer, a quick one at that.

Ronald realised that the clock has been set to zero… probably, the Red Queen's Race has started again.

SmithHan Tools: Centuries of Legacy

The Smith family has a history of centuries of tool making. They were put in-charge for the king's armory in Athena. Their core competence was tool design and manufacturing. They have been in the business for so long that their skills are emulated even by other countries. The family operated the business in an unorganised manner till around Athena's independence. They started the first mechanised factory in 1952 named as SmithHan Tools, a deformed combination of Smith and Hand Tools.

Since Athena is an agrarian economy, SmithHan's focus has always been on hand tools, meant primarily for agriculture sector. This gave them an intrinsic edge to develop the domestic market.

Geographical break-up of the business

SmithHan currently operates in nine countries apart from Athena. There are 15 manufacturing facilities across the globe. With three plants in Athena and 12 overseas, spread across nine countries, they are the biggest players in the hand tool segment. The current global market share is in the tune of 35 per cent, and revenue from overseas accounts for more than 46 per cent. SmithHan has been growing at a rate of more than 12 per cent in the last five years, mostly from geographical diversification. The revenue break-up from the domestic and overseas market is depicted in the following figure (Figure 9.1) for the current year and the last five years.

(A) Before five years

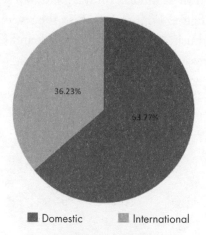

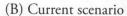

(B) Current scenario

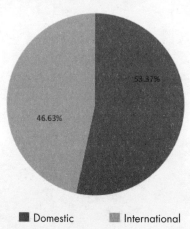

FIGURE 9.1   SmithHan Tools revenue break-up – domestic and overseas market

SmithHan Tools has mostly been focussing on the domestic market, which has been distinctly showing up in the results. As per the trend shown above, domestic market has been shrinking in the last five years, making way for the overseas market.

Product streams

Athena has a history of being an agrarian economy, and the SmithHan Tool growth story is closely linked with this history. Athena has mostly concentrated its business interest on the hand tool segment only.

The following figures (Figure 9.2) show the revenue from hand tool and machine tool business for the current year and five years before.

(A) Before five years

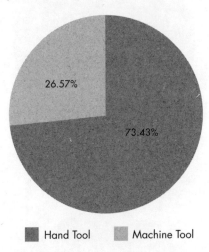
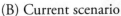

(B) Current scenario

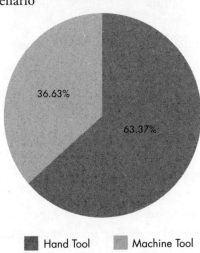

FIGURE 9.2 SmithHan Tools product-wise revenue distribution

The current revenue share of hand tools is about 63.37 per cent, which has dwindled from nearly 73.43 per cent five years before.

Logistics and Distribution of SmithHan Tools

SmithHan Tools relies on a robust distribution network for product distribution. The domestic market mainly comprises the rural areas, and this requires accessibility to the hinterlands. The overseas market mostly consists of machine tools, and the demand for hand tools is comparatively less.

The distribution is managed by two subsidiaries of SmithHan Tool – *SmithHan Logistics* and *SmithHan Logistics International*. The first one caters to the domestic market in Athena, and the second is responsible for distribution in the overseas market.

Is there a distinct shift towards machine tools?

There has been an apparent shift towards machine tools in the last few years.

Following figure (Figure 9.3) illustrates the EBITDA trend from both, hand tools and machine tools. While the EBITDA trend of hand tools is stagnant at around 12 per cent, there is an increasing trend for the machine tools. The machine tool demand has been mostly coming from the overseas market.

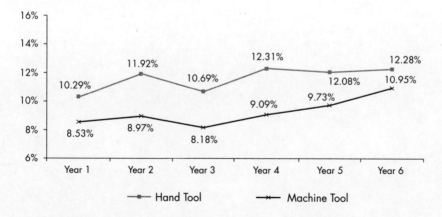

FIGURE 9.3   Smithhan Tools EBITDA trends – hand and machine tools

The Way Forward

This is a challenging situation for the SmithHan team, led by Ronald and Betty.

The Athena government has set clear focus on agricultural productivity, and this definitely requires judicious use of machine tools in the sector for boosting the efficiency. However, it also entails an increased level of awareness of machine tools amongst the agrarian community.

SmithHan clearly needs a balanced strategy that involves its experience of success of machine tools in the overseas market, knowledge of Athena market, as well as core competence of manufacturing of hand tools. An intricate choice in front of the management is to leverage on the traditional expertise, as well as to innovate to exploit the potential opportunities.

Which path should they take to achieve the objective?

PART 3

Innovation

'The Mad Hatter – 'Have I gone mad?'
Alice – 'I'm afraid so. You are entirely bonkers. But let me tell you
something, the best people usually are.'

CHAPTER 10

Innovation – A Short Primer

Defining Innovation

The subject of Innovation is protean, and so are its various notions.

Innovation, as viewed by Porter is, 'A new way of doing things (termed innovation by some authors) that is commercialised. The process of innovation cannot be separated from a firm's strategic and competitive context'.[55] The OECD Oslo Manual has defined innovation as, 'The implementation of a new or significantly improved product (good or service) or process, a new marketing method, or a new organisational method in business practices, workplace organisation, or external relations'.[54] A common feature of innovation is that it must have been implemented which signifies that the idea needs to be converted to a product or a service required by the customer.[54] Innovation can be viewed also from the perspective of a framework called Core/Context.[52] While Core represents any aspect of a company's performance that creates differentiation, Context represents everything else. According to Hamel, 'A management innovation can be defined as a marked departure from traditional management principles, processes, practices, or a departure from customary organisational forms that significantly alters the way the work of management is performed. Simply put, management innovation changes how managers do what they do."[31] In this context, innovation can span across strategy to operation, and from product to process. Hansen and Birkinshaw have mentioned that the innovation value chain in an organisation comprises steps such as – *Idea Generation, Conversion, and Diffusion.*[29]

As per Ventresca, innovation needs to be viewed as a system building activity, comprising stages of *invent, develop, innovate, transfer and consolidate, and grow and compete (IDITC).*[61] He also states that, as part of innovation strategy, while commercialising a product, an organisation needs to focus on three strategies, such as *Claiming, Demarcating, and Controlling the Market.*[60]

Govindarajan and Trimble have examined innovation from a holistic dimension beyond the realm of mere idea generation or a strong individual leadership. In this purview, innovation has been defined as 'Innovation = Idea + Leader + Team + Plan'.[24]

The definition of innovation by Freeman, and quoted by Afuah, is quite precise, concise, and specific from the perspective of desired outcome – 'Innovation is the use of new knowledge to offer a new product or service that customers want. It is Invention + Commercialisation'.[5]

This book perpends innovation from the perspective of business results. For this purpose and deducing from above, we shall base the paradigm of business innovation, defined as follows:

Innovation = Creation + Commercialisation + Business Result

We will refer to this as *Innovation Equation.* Various terms in the equation are explained below.

Creation

Creation implies anything lateral to the current way. It can be a new product (includes service) or a new process. It may be a new strategy or a new way of operation. It can pertain to a soft parameter such as motivating employees, or a tangible outcome like creation of a new product.

Commercialisation

Commercialisation connotes evaluation and development of the ideas to offerings, and subsequent execution. Execution can be implementation of the new / changed process or introduction of a product in the defined market.

Business Results

In majority of the cases, business results can be expected in terms of revenue enhancement or cost reduction. For instance, in case of introduction of a new product in a market, it will mostly result in enhancement of revenue. Implementation of a new / changed process will most likely result in cost reduction. Improving a new product may impact both – enhance revenue and reduce cost.

An innovation can nevertheless, result in an upswing in any other business metric as well. However, it is critical to link the result to revenue enhancement or cost reduction. To cite, one can quote the case of an innovation initiative to improve the motivation of employees. Even in this context, the business result may manifest itself in slowing down of attrition, which is a cost reduction for the organisation.

Societal Dimension of Innovation

It is important to note that the societal dimension of innovation, though not mentioned explicitly in the definition, can happen in two ways – explicit and implicit. First, an innovation meant for improving a business situation can address a particular need of the society. For example, a rural innovative health product launched by a healthcare chain may, apart from creating new business, uplift the health condition of the rural mass as well. The second category is when a business organisation innovates a social product, with the sole objective of improving a particular societal need. An application developed for rural youth to prepare for a competitive examination can be classified in this category.

Types of Innovation – Various Perspectives

To most people, the word innovation probably resembles the marks of a Tibetan bell. When a Tibetan bell is stuck or rubbed with a stick, it tends to peak and resonate with the same shrilling sound. Similarly, innovation, for most, tends to reverberate the extreme form of it – *a disruptive or radical innovation,* when a new product supplants an established one. However, not all innovations can harbinger the death of the old order, like the typewriter or a B & W television, or even a pager. It, as in the innovation equation, just contrives something new, that pays off in terms of business results.

It is important to view the types of innovation from the following perspectives:

(A) From the perspective of market / industry impact
(B) From the perspective of a value chain
(C) From the perspective of a product life cycle

The following discussion elaborates each perspective in detail.

(A) Market / Industry Impact Perspective

Radical or disruptive innovations and incremental innovations are the most prosaic phrases, when one tends to mention innovation. These terms intrinsically consider the fact that the market / industry have a fundamental shift or a disruption owing to the new product. This context is elaborated in the following illustration.

Radical or Disruptive Innovation

Many times, a common perspective is to equate innovation with this type, also referred many times as breakthrough innovation. According to Christensen, 'Disruptive technologies bring to market a very different value proposition than had been available previously. Generally, disruptive technologies underperform established products in mainstream markets, but that have other features that a few fringe (new) customers value. Products based on disruptive technologies are typically cheaper, simpler, and frequently more convenient to use'.[15] He has quoted transistor as an example of disruptive technology, as relative to a vacuum tube. Leifer has mentioned this category of innovation as radical innovation, and states that, 'radical innovation is a product, process, or service, with either unprecedented performance features or familiar features that offer potential for significant improvement in performance or cost. In our view, radical innovations create such a dramatic change in products, processes, or services, that they transform existing markets or industries, or create new ones.'[46] The same definition refers to the following characteristics of a radical innovation:[46]

- An entirely new set of performance features
- Improvements in known performance features of five times or greater
- A significant (30 per cent) reduction in costs

One can construe this kind of innovation from a pragmatic perspective. Disruptive innovation creates:

- Obsolescence of an existing product or product category with a new offering or
- A new market by introduction of a new product

Some examples of disruptive innovations are mobile phones with respect to pagers or CD drive that created the obsolescence of floppy drives. The most recent example is of Whatsapp or similar products like Wechat, which have been pushing traditional texting to oblivion. In the second category, we can cite Facebook that has defined the way of social interaction. Another example is of Google that created a whole new domain of Internet search, and is ever expanding to create newer territories.

Incremental Innovation

Incremental innovation refers to any improvement in the product, process, or other activities across the value chain (refer value chain perspective in the current chapter) or in the product life cycle (refer product life cycle perspective in the current chapter). In case of incremental innovations, fundamental characteristics of the existing product and markets are retained. According to Leifer, 'incremental innovation usually emphasises cost or feature improvements in existing products or services, and is dependent on exploitation competencies'.[47] One example of incremental innovation is the new features / add-ons in a software product, or even in Facebook, that enhances customer experience. Another example may be of an anti-theft software that one can add in a mobile phone.

(B) Value Chain Perspective

The value chain perspective of innovation adduces to the possible span of business innovation, i.e, it can map the functional areas where an organisation can focus to innovate.

The following (Figure 10.1) framework portrays an organisational value chain. This uses the value chain of Porter[56] as the base, with a few relevant elements added in the context of this discussion.

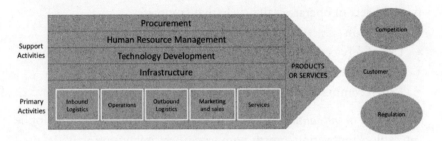

FIGURE 10.1 Value Chain

The value chain comprises primary activities as inbound logistics, operations, outbound logistics, marketing and sales, and services. The support activities are procurement, human resource management, technology management, and infrastructure. Products and services are offered to the customers. Competition and regulation constitute the environment which can influence the value chain as well as customer behaviour.

Just to refresh, in Part 2 of the book, we have illustrated three cases resembling real-life situation from three sectors. Cases are from an imaginary country Athena:

- XMobile – The largest telecom service provider in Athena
- AllHealthcare – The largest integrated healthcare provider in Athena
- SmithHan Tools – One of the top global hand tool manufacturers operating in Athena

In the following section, along with the concepts, we will use the cases of XMobile, AllHealthCare, and SmithHan Tools, to illustrate how an organisation can explore potential innovation opportunities.

(i) XMobile

PRIMARY ACTIVITIES

Innovation in inbound logistics – While there are rather more possibilities, XMobile can drive innovation across salient inbound logistics elements like network equipment supply chain, SIM card supply chain, and other outsourced partners, such as call centers and other service providers, etc.

Innovation in operations – Innovation opportunities can exist across a typical telecom operation life cycle that comprises:
- Activation
- Use of service
- Pay for use
- Exit/recommend

Innovation in outbound logistics – Outbound logistics, where XMobile can explore innovation, mostly comprises the warehousing activities used for storage of network equipment or any other material.

Innovation in marketing and sales – Innovation opportunities in marketing may involve branding, communication, and related marketing campaigns. Similarly, sales activities that mostly focus on management of the distribution channels may be another area to look for innovation opportunities.

Innovation in service – Service activities for XMobile are managed by the customer operations, which comprise the leading components of call centres and back offices (Refer Chapter 7: XMobile – Outsourcing as a Growth Strategy). These work areas offer enticing scope for potential innovation.

Secondary Activities

Innovation in Procurement – This is similar to inbound logistics and involves procurement of all equipment and services where X Mobile can drive Innovation.

Innovation in Human Resource Management – This comprises the typical cycle of hiring, nurturing, compensating and exit where XMobile can look for potential opportunities

Innovation in Technology Development – As part of its portfolio, XMobile is not involved in any technological development. However, upgradation of network or IT systems are few areas that can be explored for Innovation opportunities.

PRODUCTS/SERVICES

The current product offerings of XMobile comprise three lines of business – voice, traditional data, and new hybrid. XMobile can collaborate with external entities, or internally drive to offer new products or improve on current offerings.

MARKET/ECOSYSTEM

XMobile can explore Innovation across all the elements of market and the ecosystem – competition, customer, and regulation. Few examples of innovation in these areas may be:
- *Customer – Segmentation or micro-segmentation*
- *Competition – Sharing of resources*
- *Regulation – Creation of a structure for handling regulation*

(ii) AllHealthCare

PRIMARY ACTIVITIES

Innovation in inbound logistics – Supply chains across medicine, equipment, or even food supplies for in-patients can offer substantial scope for innovation possibilities.

Innovation in operations – The AllHealthCare product line comprises four areas of operation: in-patient, out-patient, laboratory, and research.

Innovation opportunities can be explored across in-patient care lifecycle, comprising stages of diagnosis, admission, care, investigations, billing and payment, and discharge.

Out-patient care, another area where innovation can be driven, comprises various stages as registration, examination, test (optional), etc.

Laboratory lifecycle that can be looked into from the perspective of driving innovation, may comprise sample collection / patient preparation, test and reporting, etc.

AllHealthCare research itself is directed at core innovation of new healthcare products.

Innovation in outbound logistics – AllHealthCare intrinsically does not require using any physical distribution or storage for delivery of the products or the services.

Innovation in marketing and sales – AllHealthCare can look for innovation across marketing activities, which are focussed mostly on the in-patient and out-patient care, which target the overseas patients visiting Athena for affordable quality healthcare.

Innovation in service – Service is included in the operation life cycle, as delineated above.

Secondary Activities

Innovation in procurement, human resource management – Reader may refer to the note on XMobile in the above section.

Innovation in product/services, market – For innovations in products/ services, readers may refer to the section, *Innovation in Operation* above. Readers may refer to 'Market/Ecosystem' section above, related to XMobile for market-related innovations.

(iii) SmithHan Tools

Primary Activities

Inbound logistics – Raw material for both, hand tools and machine tools are supplied by listed entities from within Athena and overseas. SmithHan adopts a traditional approach of managing the supply chain that comprises vendor listing, vendor management, vendor payment, etc., for innovation opportunities. SmithHan Tools can consider all these activities to explore innovation opportunities.

Operation – SmithHan Tools can focus on both, the lines of operations pertaining to hand tools, and machine tools, to identify innovation opportunities across products and processes.

Outbound logistics – The distribution network of SmithHan Tools is managed by its own subsidiary (refer to Chapter 9: SmithHan Tools – Logistics and Distribution). This is another area which can be looked into for innovation prospects.

Marketing and sales – Amongst others, SmithHan can focus on management of the distribution channels, both in the domestic and overseas market.

Service – While there is no direct service channel managed by SmithHan, the products are covered under warranty. Pertaining to service, SmithHan can focus on aspects that can offer innovation opportunities like product return, customer complaint management, etc.

Secondary Activities

Procurement, human resource management – This is similar to XMobile.

Technology development – Development of new and improved tools can be the part of the innovation charter of SmithHan Tools.

Product / Services

Technology development above can be referred to for the innovation opportunities in products / services area.

Market / Ecosystem

SmithHan can explore innovation mostly across competition and customer, which is similar to XMobile. Regulation is not an influencing factor in the business SmithHan is engaged in.

It is exacting to note that the description in the previous section is just an illustration of how a business organisation can explore various elements across value chain for innovation. The detailed analysis of innovation opportunities may run in few volumes, than getting contained in a few pages.

(C) Product Category Lifecycle (PLC) Perspective

While the value chain perspective can contrive the areas to look for innovation across the organisational value chain, Product Category Lifecycle can indicate the specific type of innovation, appropriate to an organisation for a particular product category. Product Category Lifecycle depicts stages of a product category, with a performance variable plotted on a timeline.[44] There are four stages (Figure 10.2) in a Product Category Lifecycle – *introduction, growth, maturity, and decline*.[33] In a traditional approach, a business organisation tends to analyse the product life cycle to devise an appropriate marketing strategy. A similar approach can be adopted too by a firm to decide on the innovation strategy as well.

We shall use the following diagram (Figure 10.2) depicting product life cycle to explain the premise.

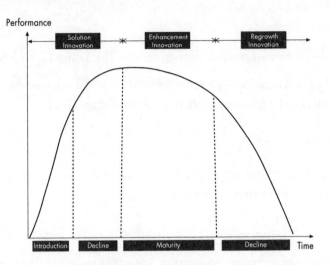

FIGURE 10.2   Product Category Life Cycle

According to Moore, one can identify about 15 various types of innovation, depending on a category life cycle.[51] As in the above depiction (Figure 10.2), in a more simplified and pragmatic approach, three basic types of innovations have been defined, based on a Product Category Life Cycle:

(a) Solution innovation
(b) Enhancement innovation
(c) Regrowth innovation

The categories cut across the product life cycle as shown in the diagram. It is critical to note that one cannot bind these in an impermeable way, and they can often overlap across the life cycle stages. The categories are discussed in the following section.

(a) Solution innovation

Solution innovation occurs during the introduction and growth stage of the product life cycle.

Solution innovation involves introduction of new products in a category, and comprises two basic types of innovation:

(i) *Product innovation*

(ii) *Application innovation.*

We shall use the following diagram (Figure 10.3) for illustrating examples from the cases.

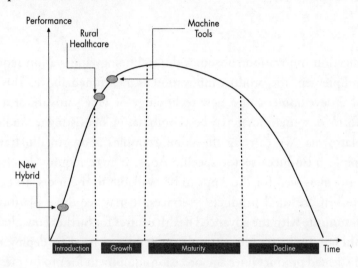

FIGURE 10.3   Introduction/growth stage products – XMobile, AllHealthcare, and SmithHan Tools

The diagram shows various products of XMobile, AllHealthcare, and SmithHan, which belong to the stages of introduction and growth. As shown, the following products are in the introduction and growth stage for the three firms:

• *XMobile – New Hybrid product is in introduction stage*

• *AllHealthCare – Rural healthcare is in early growth stage*

• *SmithHan Tools – Machine tools are in mid-growth stage*

Product innovation and application innovation are characterised in the description below, leveraging on the above examples.

(i) PRODUCT INNOVATION

Product innovation refers to development and introduction of a new product. For XMobile, considering the new hybrid products which are mostly in the late introduction and early growth stage, it should focus on introduction of new products to tap the market in this category. Similarly, AllHealthCare can rivet its efforts on product innovation in rural healthcare, which is in the introduction stage. In case of SmithHan Tools, it can direct efforts on product innovation in the machine tool category, which is in the late introduction stage in the domestic market.

(ii) Application innovation

Application innovation subsumes the technology innovation required to complement the product innovation as mentioned above. This may involve development of a new technology or new software or a new platform, or sometimes it may be a combination of existing technologies or platforms. We can tag the same examples above to illustrate. If XMobile introduces sector specific Apps, it may require developing a platform as well for the Apps to be available to the users. In case of AllHealthCare rural products / services, it may require a platform to communicate with the advanced health centres for further consultation. SmithHan Tools, for the example quoted, may need to deploy more sophisticated product lines and precision equipment for product testing.

(b) Enhancement innovation

Enhancement innovation corresponds to the maturity stage of the product life cycle. It can be construed as enhancement in features in the following dimensions:

  (i) *Product enhancement innovation*
 (ii) *Process enhancement innovation*
(iii) *Customer experience enhancement innovation*

The following diagram (Figure 10.4) illustrates the various products of XMobile, AllHealthCare, and SmithHan Tools, which are in the maturity stage:

- *XMobile – Vvoice products*
- *AllHealthcare – In-patient care*
- *SmithHan Tools – Hand tools*

We will refer to this for illustration from the cases.

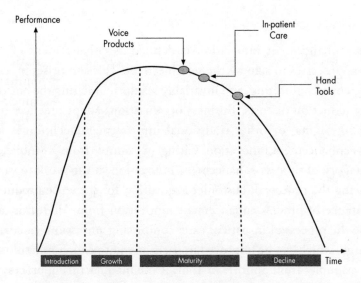

FIGURE 10.4 Maturity stage products – XMobile, AllHealthcare, and SmithHan Tools

The following section is a description of all four categories in enhancement innovations.

(i) Product enhancement innovation

Product enhancement innovation encompasses enhancement of features of the existing product. Citing the example from XMobile, voice product currently resides in the region of maturity, making it a good candidate for product enhancement innovation. One example of product enhancement for voice product may be of bundling of the data or a new hybrid product. Referring to AllHealthCare in-patient care, which is in the maturity stage, there is potential to enhance the features of the services in this category. An instance of product enhancement in this case may be of loyalty discount or combining in-patient care with home care after discharge of the patient. For SmithHan Tools, hand tools lie in the region of maturity, and we can examine the case of hand files belonging to this category. SmithHan can probably apply the technique of value engineering to change the product constituents, so that functionality can be augmented.

(ii) PROCESS ENHANCEMENT INNOVATION

Process enhancement innovation is defined as enhancement of the business processes to achieve the set objectives. This comprises process redesign or reengineering, and invariably results in inflating the bottom line by reduction of costs. Business organisations adopt practices like Lean, Six Sigma, or other traditional improvement techniques for process enhancement innovation. Citing an example from XMobile, in the category of process enhancement innovation, it can work towards enhancing the process of customer acquisition for the voice products. An instance of process enhancement innovation from AllHealthCare may be the process of in-patient care, comprising admission, care, and discharge, which can be improved in parts or end to end. Similarly, one of the examples from SmithHan Tools is the manufacturing process of hand files, which can be attempted for enhancement. Pertaining to this, there may be enhancements like line balancing, continuous flow, etc., to enhance the manufacturing process.

(iii) CUSTOMER EXPERIENCE ENHANCEMENT INNOVATION

The focal point of customer experience enhancement innovation is enhancement of customer experience. This is primarily achieved through improvement of the supporting services of the main line of product. For instance, XMobile can work towards improving the resolution time of customer complaints to improve customer experience. Quoting the example of AllHealthCare, they may call a super specialist, or say, a psychotherapist, free of cost, for the admitted patients, which is likely to augment the customer experience. SmithHan Tools can initiate a dedicated service line, or create special warranty schemes, etc.

(C) Regrowth innovation

Regrowth innovation can be tagged to the decline stage of the product life cycle when the market shrinks to inoperable minimum. This entails an organisation to look at innovation from the perspective of renewal. Regrowth innovation can happen in the following directions:

   (i) *Category renewal innovation*

(ii) *Market renewal innovation*

(iii) *Acquisition innovation*

The following section delineates the types in detail.

(i) CATEGORY RENEWAL INNOVATION

Category renewal innovation refers to when an organisation develops and introduces a different category of products within its core competence. In fact, this harbingers the start of another new product life cycle. For example, if a particular voice product market saturates (e.g., a voice product aimed at health professionals), XMobile can explore introducing a new product category (e.g., a special voice product for students). Citing an example for AllHealthCare, it can probably introduce a product as in-patient old-age healthcare, when the in-patient market starts declining. For SmithHan, focus on the machine tools is an example of category renewal innovation.

(ii) MARKET RENEWAL INNOVATION

Market renewal innovation pertains to when an organisation forays into a new market, with the product entering into the decline phase in the existing market. The new market may be different geographically, or it may be a different segment. For example, XMobile, with the small towns and semi-rural markets getting saturated, can venture into rural market with the same voice product. AllHealthCare foraying into rural is another illustration of market renewal innovation. Similarly, with hand tool market in Athena getting saturated, SmithHan can try to set foot in some other market.

(iii) ACQUISITION INNOVATION

Acquisition Innovation is when an organisation acquires a suitable partner on decline of a particular category in the existing market. The acquired partner may be a new entrant, with strong hold on the particular product line know-how, or it may be an old player with substantial share of the market. Facebook's acquisition of WhatsApp (2014) and Oculus (2014) are apt examples of acquisition innovation.

S-Curve – Predicting Technology Obsolescence

The Apocalypse

To remain competitive in the market, business firms need to be fully abreast of the life path of the underlying technology of the product offerings. Compared with product life cycle, Sigmoid Curve, referred commonly as S-Curve,[4,34,35] is apocalyptical in the sense that it is effective to assess and predict life cycle of a technology. S-Curve, in an ideal scenario, follows the pattern, as in the Figure 10.5 below.

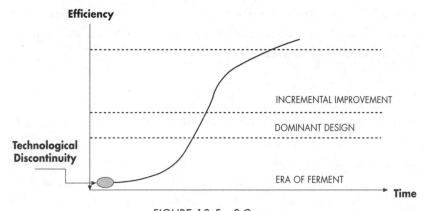

FIGURE 10.5   S-Curve

The basic construct of S-Curve comprises plotting relevant performance criteria (e.g., speed, capacity, etc.) in a time scale. As depicted in the curve, one can detect four significant zones / points in the life trajectory of a technology[59] – *technological discontinuity, era of ferment, dominant design, and era of incremental change.*

Technological discontinuity

This commences with the introduction of competence destroying or competence enhancing technology. Technological discontinuities are 'those rare, unpredictable innovations, that advance a technological frontier by an order of magnitude, and which involve fundamentally different product or process design, and that commands a decisive cost, performance, or quality advantage over product forms'.[59] Technological discontinuity also signals the death of an existing technology, and the related product in most of the cases.

Era of ferment

Intense design competition occurs during this phase, with the emergence of various product options, with each one following various technical approaches.

Dominant design

Dominant design represents the winner in a product category or class. According to Geroski, Dominant designs are:[21]

- Consensus good – An effective compromise of needs of large sections of customer, both current and potential.
- Nexus good – Identifies the complementary needs, and also specifies how to hook these to the core product.
- Platform good – Acts as a generic template

Era of Incremental change

Emergence of a dominant design harbingers the inception of the 'era of incremental change'. This is the stage when the product undergoes incremental improvements of various orders and forms, while the fundamental design considerations remain intact.

The era of incremental change ends with the advent of another technological discontinuity, with the emergence of a new S-Curve.

S-Curve illustrative example – Mobile Phones

We can illustrate S-Curve with the example of evolution of mobile phones, as in the following diagram (Figure 10.6)

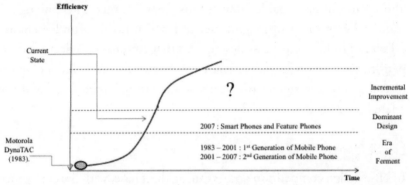

FIGURE 10.6   S-Curve for mobile phones

While the cellular technology has emerged through years, launch of DynaTAC by Motorola in 1983 signified the *technological discontinuity*, spelling the death knell on pager industry. The time period from 1983 to 2007 can be adduced as the *era of ferment*, which has seen intense competition with the introduction of new phones in two phases.[9,50] The first generation can be marked in the year between 1983 to 2001, and comprised analog-based bulky handsets, equipped mostly with voice handling capability. Operating systems were wide and varied, and were in nascent stages in terms of technological maturity. The second generation genesis can be traced back to 2001, which was conspicuous by handsets with efficient texting and other capability. Handsets became sleeker, and multimedia handling capability was introduced around the year 2003. The inception of the *dominant design* phase can be marked with the introduction of iPhone by Apple in 2007. While this is still evolving, one can notice two dominant designs in the fray – *smart phones* and *feature phones*. Smart phones are characterised by standard operating systems (mostly iOS and Android), touch screen, and a similar layout of the operating menus. Many consider feature phones as just a retronym, and can be distinguished by less advanced features than a smart phone with proprietary operating system.[50] Quoting KPMG report on mobile evolution, 'Platform markets generally standardise to two or three. In mobile, Apple and Android™ currently dominate at around 80 per cent market share. Yes; Android is the clear winner in terms of unit sales, but Apple is still the number one when it comes to value – either from revenue generated by applications, e-commerce commissions, and web traffic.'[45] The current trend of handset market indicates a clear consumer shift towards the smart phone, with its sale clearly exceeding feature phone sale in the year 2013. Predicated on the trend, it is rationale to infer that, in time to come, smart phones is likely to establish itself as the winning *dominant design*. Era of incremental improvement will follow the same; and yes, in the days to come, it will be interesting to see if an open system like Android can dethrone iOS, even in terms of value as well.

Transilience Map – Determining Organisational Capabilities to drive Innovation

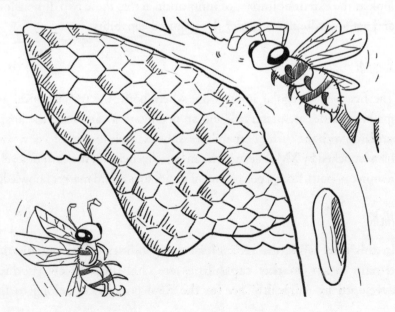

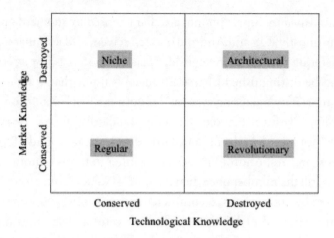

FIGURE 10.7   Transilience Map

Transilience Map propounded by Abernathy and Clarke (Figure 10.7) can assist an organisation to determine the managerial and technical traits required to nurture in the face of innovations of various kinds.[2] The framework is depicted in the above figure.

The framework specifies two kinds of organisational capabilities: *technological knowledge* and *market knowledge,* which can get influenced due to a specific innovation. As the model suggests, an organisation can look at the extent of impact of innovation across these two dimensions, and act accordingly to garner the required capability.

Regular

The first one is regular innovation, where both, the technological and market abilities are preserved, and an organisation can tackle the arising situation with the current capabilities. One example may be of a new voice plan launched by XMobile, which can be delivered with the current level of resources – both, from a perspective of technological and market knowledge.

Niche

In this case, while the technological capabilities of the organisation remain intact, market capabilities are challenged. New products developed by AllHealthCare for the rural population belong to this category where the organisation mostly needs to develop new capability in market-related activities.

Revolutionary

With reference to this category, there is no impact on the market-related capability, but the technological capability is challenged. Quoting an example from SmithHan Tools, a new kind of hand tool might be an example where the organisation needs to acquire new technology to develop it. It can depend on the current market ability to penetrate the market, assuming that the tool will address the needs of a current segment of customer.

Architectural

Both, technological and market-related abilities are challenged in case of innovation of this type. We can quote the example from XMobile if it decides to enter into the domain of providing Internet services. This would entail XMobile to develop capabilities in both, the dimensions of technology and market.

Innovation Ecosystem — A Synopsis

Perseus and Gorgons lair[38]

Perseus, the great mythological Greek warrior, was the progeny of Zeus, the father of Gods and men, who rules from Mount Olympus. Polydectus, the king of Seriphos offered young Perseus the challenge to bring the head of Gorgon Medusa. Medusa was a dreaded female monster and could turn anybody to stone with just a gaze. Perseus was the progeny of the king of the Gods, but Medusa was just impossible to defeat – she was invincible.

According to scriptures, an arduous expedition starts and Perseus embarks on the journey, seeking help from various Gods and other creatures. Hermes gives him the winged sandal that enables him to fly. A sickle was also given for slaying Medusa's neck. Athena, sister of Hermes, offered him a shield, so that Medusa's image can be reflected without getting turned into stone. On advice from Hermes and Athena, Perseus goes to the cave of the Graeae (three strange women with only one eye amongst them, which they constantly fight over) who inform him about the Nymphs of the North. When Perseus meets them, the Nymphs of the North offer him the Cap of Darkness that makes the wearer invisible. Perseus was also blessed by them with a magic wallet for keeping Medusa's head.

Equipped with the armoury, Perseus now flies using the winged sandal to Gorgons' Lair, the den of Medusa. He kills the monster after a fierce fight, and the victor sets off for the shores of Seriphos.

This story of Perseus semaphores best what an innovation ecosystem is and how it works.

To explain the same, we shall first depict the story in the following diagram (Figure 10.8).

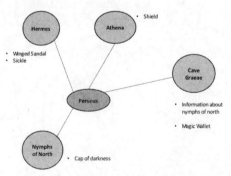

FIGURE 10.8   Story of Perseus – Diagrammatic Illustration

As seen, we can identify a few elements in the story. Perseus is the *actor* who collaborates with various *entities* to meet his objective. There is an exchange of material *resource* or *information*. With any of the linkages in the network broken, it would have made Perseus unsuccessful in his attempt to slay Medusa.

Innovation Ecosystem

Innovation ecosystem refers to the connected congregation of entities (e.g. researchers, institutions, etc.), which are required to work in a coherent way to drive innovation from the invention to the marketplace. According to a report by the US President's Council of Advisors on Science and Technology, in the context of a country, innovation ecosystem is 'the dynamic system of interconnected institutions and persons that are necessary to propel technological and economic development'.[20] Ron Adner has defined innovation ecosystem as the 'collaborative arrangements through which firms combine their individual offerings into a coherent, customer-facing solution.'[3] The entities may include the material resources (funds, equipment, facilities, etc.), the human capital (students, faculty, staff, industry researchers, industry representatives, etc.) and institutional entities (e.g., the universities, colleges of engineering, business schools, business firms, venture capitalists (VC), industry-university research institutes, federal or industrial supported centres of excellence, and state and/or local economic development and business assistance organisations, funding agencies, policy makers, etc.).[43]

Connectedness to the innovation ecosystem plays a crucial role when a firm decides to take an invention to the marketplace. To illustrate, let us assume that XMobile is trying to launch a mobile app that can predict the weather at a village level, and is targeted at the rural farmers. The innovation ecosystem for the particular innovation can be depicted as shown in Figure 10.9.

While XMobile remains at the hub of the initiative, there are entities which are critical to its success. Solution design or the product design is dependent on the universities, research institutes, etc., that can provide the technology. Development of the solution to create an App is done

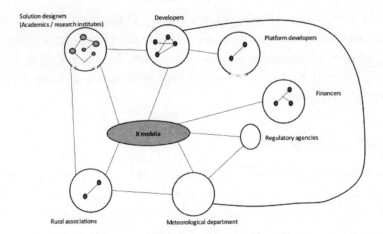

FIGURE 10.9   Innovation Ecosystem – Illustrative

by developers. The platform refers to the common digital platform like Google Play Store where the Apps resides. The financiers are VCs or other financial institutions required for funding the commercialisation of the product. Considering the weather application, it would require data feeding from the meteorological department. Similarly, XMobile may have to tie-up with rural associations, etc., to create the early adopters of the product.

As can be perceived by the examples, similar to the story of Perseus, the innovation ecosystem comprises entities from various orbits, and each plays a specific role, from conceptualisation / design, till successful commercialisation.

According to Ron Adner, there are three kinds of risks in relation with an innovation ecosystem.[3]

- **Initiative risks** – This includes traditional uncertainties associated with the management of a project. Initiative risks comprise product feasibility, customer benefit, appropriateness of supply chain, etc.
- **Interdependence risks** – Interdependence risk refers to the risks associated with the dependencies associated with dealing with the other components of the innovation ecosystem.
- **Integration risks** – The risks associated with the adoption process across the value chain are defined as integration risks.

An organisation, while interacting with the related innovation ecosystem, is required to equip itself to deal with the particular kind of risk or any possible combination.

Role of People in driving Innovation in a Business Organisation

Roles for driving innovation

While structures, processes, and technologies are the blood and sinews, people represent the soul of a successful innovation. The right ingredient of it or the lack of one can elevate an innovation initiative to the level of sustenance, or push it into oblivion.

Govindarajan and Trimble has recognised three basic principles, while creating a dedicated team, and this involves identification of the required skills, hiring the best people, and matching the organisational model to the dedicated team's responsibilities.[25]

Based on the essence of innovation, one can view three different fundamental roles, vital for an organisation to remain innovative – *sketchers, developers, and executors.* One can model them in line with the construction of a high rise. *Sketchers* are idea or concept generators. They are like the ones who generate the sketch or probably the blueprint of a high rise.

Developers convert the concept/idea to a workable solution. This resembles the architect who converts the blueprint to a three-dimensional design, with all the design parameters to make it live. The last category is *executors,* who implement the designed solution with commercial success. Again, this mirrors the role of a civil engineer who converts the design into reality.

Afuah has mentioned five different kinds of roles that are vital in a successful innovation initiative[6]:

- **Idea generators** – *Individuals who can churn information to generate ideas for a successful product.*
- **Gatekeepers and boundary spanners** – Gatekeepers and boundary spanners act as the transducers for inter-firm and intra-firm information.
- **Champions** – Champions are profiles in an organisation who drive the innovation effort with all the might at their disposal, and go beyond the traditional responsibilities to achieve success.
- **Sponsors** – They are senior level members in the organisation who guide, mentor, and support the innovation initiatives.
- **Project managers** – Project managers plan and support the execution of the initiatives.

Complementary to the roles, it is also imperative for an organisation to take cognizance of the core skills required for innovation. One can identify the following five qualities which are mentioned as the DNA that an innovator needs to possess.[18]

- **Associating** – Ability to put or combine ideas together.
- **Questioning** – Creative imagination to ask the right questions.
- **Observing** – Intense capability to observe to know what works and what doesn't.
- **Networking** – Ability to get insight from resources, both within and outside traditional networks.
- **Experimenting** – Risk-taking ability to experiment with the idea that answers the 'what-if' questions, and generate data for future course of action.

Vices that hinder innovation

Probably, this quote from a 1960 movie *Heller in Pink Tights* outlines the vital role that an individual can play in a successful innovation,

'*You got trails where you take one wrong step and you're over the edge.*' One wrong foot and the soul veers to a wrong path…you're doomed in your innovation journey. It is important for the HR manager to identify and put the right resources with traits that foster innovation. While it is easier to enlist the antonyms of the above list of DNAs as the vices that hinder innovation, the most common ones that will top the list are close-mindedness and over confidence, based on past performance. Anthony D Scott has also referred few deadly sins that highlight the common mistakes by an innovator.[7]

- Pride – Perception-based judgment to push a product to the market.
- Sloth – Slow pace of innovation initiative to reach customers.
- Lust – Distraction to follow 'too many bright shiny objects'.
- Greed – Trying to earn too much in too little time without right prioritisation.

  The right personnel in the right roles to drive innovation could be a game changer in the marketplace for any organisation.

Open Innovation

Open innovation is the buzzword doing the rounds in business circles quite noticeably. This section delineates the concept of open innovation, along with the critical features.

What is open innovation

The current socio-business environment, as mentioned by Chesbrough, can be appropriately paraphrased by this quote from Charles Dickens – 'it is the best of the times, it is the worst of the times' for innovation.[14] The following two illustrations that characterise the digital age reflect the situation aptly.

(a) Speed of Digital Evolution – Moore's Law

The digital revolution in terms of processing speed and degree of connectedness are two vital factors that significantly influence the competitiveness of a firm. The digital processing power is improving at a breakneck speed. As per Moore's law, digital processor speeds, or overall processing power for computers will double every two years.[39]

This adjures that an organisation needs to ride on the leading edge of the digital wave, and needs to look beyond the internal capabilities to remain innovative.

(b) Technology Adoption Time

Technology adoption time has reduced drastically in case of digital, or more in case of Internet-based products. For instance, for reaching a diffusion of 25 per cent (per cent of ownership) radios took more than 25 years. However, in case of Internet, it took even less than 10 years to reach the same figure.[22] In case of WhatsApp, it took just four years to reach a customer base of more than 400 million, while Facebook during the same time could reach a customer base of 150 million only.[36]

The environment, dictated by the speed and scale of digital connect, has rendered the business firms to drive innovation with a perspective lateral to a traditional one, and explore beyond organisational boundaries. One can relate this to genesis of open innovation.

'Open innovation' according to Chesbrough, who has coined this term, 'is a paradigm that assumes that firms can and use external ideas as well as internal ideas, and internal and external paths to market, as the firms looks to advance their technology.'[13] As per him, 'Open innovation assumes that the internal ideas can be taken to market through external channels, outside the current businesses of the firm, to generate additional value.'[13]

There are three facets one needs to consider, while deploying an open innovation in an organisation.[48]

- The ideas are generated in different contexts, and hence, are different than those generated within the organisation.
- The external sources also can be utilised as the last-mile conduit to take the ideas to market.
- The internal resources who has already worked in the concept of Open Innovation in some form (marketing etc.) should be used to remind the organization to expect 'the known' rather than 'the unknown'

Seidel has mentioned (based on Howe, 2006 and Boudreau & Lekhani, 2009) few vital design components (Table 10.1) of an Open Innovation system.[58]

TABLE 10.1   Design Components of an Open Innovation System

Design of community dynamic
1. Contributors: Who are the target members of the community
2. Access: How do members learn about and gain access to the community
3. Relationship: Are members to collaborate or to compete?
4. Governance: How is behaviour in the community managed?
5. Motivation: What is a member's motivation to participate?
6. Task: How are the tasks made modular and clear to members?

Design of firm's absorptive capacity
7. Filters: How will ideas be evaluated and by whom?:
8. Integration: How will ideas be tested and further developed by the firm?
9. Platform: Does the firm serve as final integrator or serve as an open product platform?

Open Innovation Examples

Google's Android operating system is one of the best examples of an open innovation. It is open to millions of developers across the globe for creating their apps. Play store is the market for distributing the products.

Another oft-quoted example of open innovation is *Connect & Develop* program nurtured by Procter & Gamble. *Connect & Develop* comprised creating an innovation network with the relevant entities (e.g. entrepreneurs, individuals, etc.) and to tap the potential ideas. Huston and Sakkab mentioned,[41] 'With a clear sense of consumer needs, we could identify promising ideas throughout the world and apply our own R&D, manufacturing, marketing, and purchasing capabilities to them, to create better and cheaper products, faster.' The results were phenomenal. From 2000 to 2006, 35 per cent of the P&G products had some elements developed outside. During the same time, R&D productivity increased by about 60 per cent and the R&D cost as percentage of investment, has reduced from 4.8 per cent to 3.4 per cent. Also, more importantly, the share price doubled during this period.[38]

The realm of open innovation is expanding faster, and in the years to come, more and more companies would feel the need to venture into this domain.

Measurement of Innovation

If not to heaven, as in this quote from Shakespeare, '*Ignorance is the curse of God; knowledge is the wing wherewith we fly to heaven*', measurement of innovation can put a firm in the right stride. While there are hypotheses on how to assess innovation capability, these are not standardised and have not attained an industry-wide acceptance.

Gupta has mentioned five levels of innovation maturity in an organisation, referred to as BIMM.[30] While the work delineates the levels, the method of determination has not been deliberated in detail.

I²MM (Integrated Innovation Maturity Model)[57] is another framework by Prothmann and Stein, where five levels of organisation

maturity have been mentioned: *chaotic, organised, standardised, predictable, and black belt.* The levels have been proposed across four process areas namely: *ideation and product development, innovation management, requirement engineering, and quality management.* The model is silent on how to measure the achievement levels.

The works of Essmann and Preez[19] are commendable in this area where the drivers of innovation have been viewed from three perspectives: *organisational construct, innovation capability construct, and capability maturity.* Based on the same, five levels of innovation maturity have been referred: *Ad hoc, defined, supported, aligned, and synergised.*

Works of Booz & Co[10] have listed four basic areas in the innovation capability of an organisation: *ideation, project selection, product development, and commercialisation.* Top parameters in these areas are: *customer insights and analytics, understanding of technology trends/ ongoing assessment of market potential, project resource requirement forecasting and planning/ engagement with customer to prove real-world feasibility, product platform management/ pilot user selection, and product-life cycle management.* The measurement is perception based rather than through an assessment of the drivers across a company.

ADL's *Innovation Excellence Performance Areas*[8] is another model used to measure organisational innovation. While the model is very specific on financial performance as sales, ebit, and break-even with respect to new products/services, the measurement is survey based which implies that the assessment is done based on the perception based estimation rather than depending on hard evidences.

Though not from the domain of innovation, the cue on measuring capability and maturity can be taken from few other models. SEI CMM[11] has defined five levels of organisational maturity: *initial, managed, defined, quantitatively managed, and optimising.* Similarly, COPC is very robust on measuring results, and has defined specific metrics.[16] In measuring the capability, Malcolm Baldrige adopts a structured scale which is worth looking at.[53]

Real-life Cases

In the following section, we will discuss three cases to illustrate how a business firm becomes Innovative to remain competitive in the market. The discussed cases are on Apple, 3M, and Google.

(A) Apple

Apple's capability to innovate is built on an innovation factory[65] as shown in the following figure.

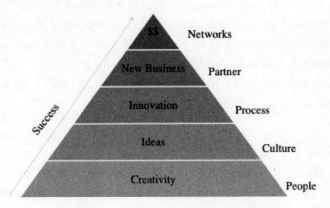

FIGURE 10.10   Apple Innovation Framework

The essence of innovation in Apple can be summarised by the following:

(a) Ability to read the market

Apple's ability to read the market is exemplary and echoed by this statement of Steve Jobs, 'There is an old Wayne Gretzky quote that I love. "I skate to where the puck is going to be, not where it has been". And we have always tried to do that in Apple. Since the very beginning. And we always will.'[64]

(b) Visionary Leadership

Through the visionary leadership, Steve Jobs was able to create a balanced system of products, always keeping people in perspective. During a joint interview in 2007 at the 'All Things Digital Conference', Bill Gates mentioned, 'I'd seen Steve make the decision based on a sense of people and product that, you know, is hard for me to explain. The way he does things is different, and I think, it is magical. And, in that case, Wow'.[42]

(c) Investing in the right people

Apple has been able to assemble the right set of people for the right kinds of jobs, creating a balanced system of creativity and delivery. Dalal (2012) has mentioned, 'Apple has assembled some of the best innovators and leaders under one roof; from industrial engineering to retail, software engineering to mobile, all working in synch to create breakthrough products. Most of these leaders have been with Apple since late nineties, and have created a core group that could rival the CEOs of most companies.'[17]

(d) Connectedness with the Ecosystem

Other factors contributing to Apple's ability to innovate are its strong ties with the ecosystem, and being able to co-create value. Taking the example of an iPad, the value is being created by a set of independent app developers, as well as various content providers, etc. Quoting Ventresca (2011), *'It is a value creation by assembly of heterogeneous drivers.'*[62]

(e) Performance Focus

Performance focus has been at the apex of the Apple's innovation strategy. It is illustrated by the facts that by 2008, in just over a decade, the revenue has increased by 1200 per cent, and the net profit soared by more than 3000 per cent.[17]

(B) 3M

The innovation capability of 3M is illustrated by the fact that about the year 2000, 30 per cent of its sales used to come from products new to the market.[27]

The 3M way of innovation is built around 3M's innovation wheel as below (Figure 10.11).[28]

The underlying factors which characterise innovation in 3M are illustrated by the following characteristics:

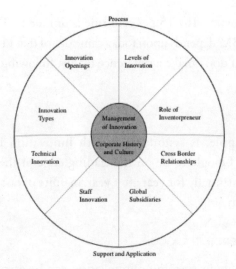

Process

Innovation Openings

Levels of Innovation

Innovation Types

Management of Innovation

Role of Inventorpreneur

Corporate History and Culture

Technical Innovation

Cross Border Relationships

Staff Innovation

Global Subsidiaries

Support and Application

FIGURE 10.11   3M's Wheel of Innovation

(a) Strong Process of Innovation

There is an underlying process governing innovation in 3M. The process clearly defines the *types of innovation, ways to innovate (innovation openings), levels of innovation, and the role of the inventropreneurs (outstanding innovators).*

(b) Defined Support and Application

A strong support system enables the defined process. It has its focus on *technical innovation, staff innovation, relationships with global subsidiaries, and other cross border entities exploiting across the value chain.*

(c) Strong Innovation Culture

Another significant factor defining the innovation capability of 3M is a culture conducive to innovation. As per Roger Appledorn (2000), there are few factors which characterise innovation culture in 3M: *recognising heroes, freedom to express, excitement and anticipation, never give up, giving value to failure, and fun.*[29] Another noteworthy fact is the 15 Per cent Rule[40] which allows employees to spend 15 per cent of work hours playing with ideas.

Quoting Bill Coyne, 'The 15 per cent rule is unique to 3M. Most of the inventions that 3M depends upon today came out of that kind of individual initiative ... You don't make a difference by just following orders.'[1]

(C) Google

Google, like Apple, is synonymous with innovation for many. It is amazing to see Google to be on the leading edge of the path-defining innovations continually for year after year, in-spite of fast-paced changes in the ecosystem.

Innovation Essence in Google

Success of Google in sustaining innovation can be attributed to a few factors:[37]
- *Platform and ecosystem-based innovation*
- *Continuous improvement in infrastructure*
- *Radical adjacencies to become more integrated (deliveries) and to look for a new disruption (e.g. Google glass, driverless car etc.)*
- *Device innovations, which are proving difficult to generate, along with supply chains that it lacks experience of*
- *Design centric focus*
- *Bench-time – a factor most companies now deprive their engineers of*

In essence, innovation in Google is dependent on openness to the external world and nurturing an innovation-friendly culture.

Google Innovation Pillars

'Nurturing a culture that allows for innovation is the key. As we've grown to over 26,000 employees in more than 60 offices, we've worked hard to maintain the unique spirit that characterised Google way back when I joined as employee #16', mentions Susan Wojcicki, former senior vice president of Google. In reference to which path Google decided to tread in the journey of innovation, she has remarked, 'What's different is that, even as we dream up what's next, we face the classic innovator's dilemma: should we invest in brand new products, or should we improve existing ones? We believe in doing both, and learning while we do it.'

According to Susan, Google's innovation structure is based on eight pillars, as illustrated below.[63]

(a) Have a mission that matters

One can compare mission to a lighthouse – you look at it when you are lost in the sea. All of Google's decisions are guided by the mission, 'organise the world's information, and make it universally accessible and useful.'

(b) Think big but start small

However big the future might be, the start may be in small steps. One instance is of Google Books, which brings millions of books online. While it looked like a crazy idea to many even to conceive, Larry Page started this by using a scanner to experiment how much time may be required to load a book on search. Today, hundreds of millions of books are available in Google Books.

(c) Strive for continual innovation, not instant perfection

Innovation can't happen overnight, and there is an iterative process that runs deep in Google initiatives. It relies on 'watching users on wild', learning based on data, and taking the next step faster and quicker.

(d) Look for ideas everywhere

Google relies on an 'unstructured structure' that inherently captures ideas from both, internal and external sources. Quoting Susan, 'Some of the best ideas at Google are sparked just like that – when small groups of Googlers take a break on a random afternoon, and start talking about things that excite them.'

(e) Share everything

Google has a culture of sharing information, and employees are mostly aware of what is happening around. This encourages exchange of ideas and enhances innovation. Even the employees sit in crowded teams in cubicles which facilitates discussion.

(f) Spark with imagination, fuel with data

Google believes in offering beyond what the customers may not even imagine. Right resources who believe that the impossible can be achieved are recruited with preference. Blue sky thinking is encouraged in Google 20 per cent of time, i.e. on one full day in a week, engineers can wish to work on whatever they want.

(g) Be a platform

Google believes in openness, and acts as a hub to tap the potential of millions of innovators across the word. The best example is the Android OS, which is contributed by millions of developers across the globe, and the developers are supported by Google's extensive resources.

(h) Never fail to fail

Google is never afraid of failure. It tolerates failure, as long as there is learning for the future. Susane has mentioned about a project *Google Answers,* which was started along with AdSense. While AdSense has grown to be a multi-billion dollar business, *Google Answers* was called off after four years. However, the learnings were applied for the development of future products.

Google X – The Moonshot Factory[26]

How many business firms can, in the real sense, come out of the cliché of making tonnes of money, and just dare to focus on creating value for the customer first, and to figure out ways to make money later? While Google is just doing that, Google X is an aspiring extension. Google X is about making a problem 10 times better, with a timeframe of 10 years. It is about making huge transformative and disruptive changes. This is happening in Google's dedicated research laboratory, away off from the main campus – there is no sign to tell where you are. Astro Teller, Captain of Moonshot designated says, 'If we manage to succeed with even one of the projects we're working on here, we won't need a sign'. One such transformational project is driverless cars that don't crash. The concept has already clocked hundreds of thousands of miles. This quote from Astro Teller summarises it all, 'If you don't reward failure, people will hang on to a doomed idea for the fear of consequences. That wastes time and saps an organisation's spirit.'

Connecting with ICaM – next sections

Professed by numerous researches, including the one on which this book is based and successful innovation examples, it is amply clear that business innovation doesn't happen by chance. It imperatively calls for a structured approach, one crafted either by a conscious design, or that is underlying the visible layers of a company due to the way it works. According to Govindarajan and Trimble, 'In all great innovation stories, the great idea is only Chapter 1.'[23]

As evinced through the previous discussions, innovation in an organisation needs to be founded on a few basic ingredients:

- A directional intent on innovation
- Knowledge of the related underlying technologies
- An apocalyptical sense of the market
- Right people in the right place
- Connectedness with the appropriate entities of the ecosystem at the appropriate stage of innovation
- Strong linkage with business metrics

The maxims form the brass tacks of the ICaM framework, which is the core of the book. In the subsequent sections, the framework is discussed in detail, along with the approach and illustration of application.

PART 4

Structure of Business Innovation – ICaM

'The rule is, jam tomorrow and jam yesterday-but never jam today'.
'It must come sometime to jam today', Alice objected
'No it can't', said the Queen. 'It's jam every other day. Today isn't any other
day, you know'.

CHAPTER 11

Structure of ICaM

ICaM Framework

Figure 11.1 below illustrates the structure and composition of the ICaM Framework.

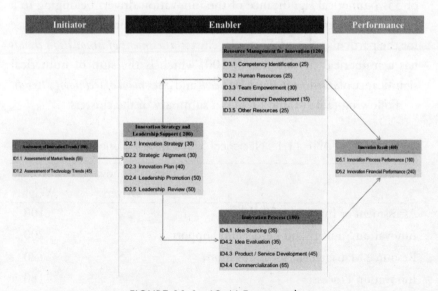

FIGURE 11.1   ICaM Framework

Definition of Elements of the Framework

(A) Innovation Drivers

Innovation drivers refers to the element / activities a business firm needs to focus to drive innovation, e.g., *assessment of market needs,* etc. There are 18 innovation drivers in total. Each innovation driver is denoted with an identification prefix 'ID' (an acronym for innovation driver).

(B) Clusters

Similar innovation drivers are grouped into one class, referred to as 'cluster'. Example, *assessment of market needs* and *assessment of technology trends* are grouped into a cluster named as *assessment of innovation trends.* There are five clusters in total.

(C) Numerical Significance

Numerical significance refers to the numerical weights of the innovation drivers. Example, *assessment of market needs* has a numerical significance of 55. Numerical significance of the innovation drivers belonging to a particular cluster rolled up together, represents the numerical significance for the particular cluster. Example, cluster *assessment of innovation trends* has a numerical significance of 100, which is the sum of numerical significance of *assessment of market needs* and *assessment of technology trends.*

Following table (Table 11.1) is a summary of the clusters:

TABLE 11.1   Numerical Significance – Clusters

Cluster	No. of Innovation Drivers	Total Weights
Assessment of Innovation Trends	2	100
Innovation Strategy and Leadership Support	5	200
Resource Management for Innovation	5	120
Innovation Process	4	180
Innovation Results	2	400
	Total	1,000

Cluster Snapshots

Assessment of Innovation Trends

This cluster depicts the requirements a business firm needs to assess, with respect to current trends in innovation, prior to strategy formulation. Numerical significance of the cluster is 100, and there are two innovation drivers.

Innovation Strategy and Leadership Support

Innovation strategy and leadership support defines what a business firm needs to focus with respect to defining the strategy to drive innovation, as well as the kind and degree of support by senior leadership. Numerical significance of 200 is distributed across five innovation drivers in this cluster.

Resource Management for Innovation

Management of resources, both human and other resources, while driving innovation, is construed in this cluster. Five innovation drivers constitute this cluster, with a numerical significance of 120.

Innovation Process

A structured process that a business firm can adopt to drive innovation is the focal point of this cluster. There are four innovation drivers, with a total numerical significance of 180.

Innovation Results

It is vital to link the innovation efforts with business results, and this cluster sketches out various metrics for it. A numerical significance of 400 is assigned to this cluster, with two innovation drivers.

How were the Innovation Drivers determined, Clusters formed, and Numerical Significance decided?

As mentioned in Part 1, the work is based on the research of the author as part of the Post Graduate Programme in Strategy and Innovation from the University of Oxford (2013). Extensive industry and relevant research was done to further consolidate the findings. Validation was done with application and testing of the framework in few firms across spectrum of sectors. The background research comprised industry research, expert interviews, and statistical analysis on the findings, and rendered the determination of innovation drivers, formation of clusters, and decision on numerical significance.

The next section delineates the innovation drivers one by one.

CHAPTER 12

Assessment of Innovation Trends

Assessment of innovation trends is a critical element to initiate any innovation effort in a business firm. This assessment has two dimensions – *assessment of market needs* and *assessment of technology trends*.

Driver Requirements – Assessment of Innovation Trends

ID 1.1 Assessment of Market Needs
- The organization should deploy ways and means to know the market needs from both customers and non-customers, to determine innovation needs and trends applicable to it.
- The gained knowledge should be translated to determine the innovation needs in the current and future context, and applicable/appropriate in the context of the organisation.

ID 1.2 Assessment of Technology Trends
- The organisation should deploy ways to have a detailed understanding of the emerging technology trends appropriate to it.
- The understanding should lead to an assessment of the role of innovation in the competitive positioning, as well as guide the strategic focus required by the organisation in the perspective of innovation needs.

CHAPTER 13

Strategy and Leadership Support

It is imperative for a firm to convert the innovation requirement determined from the previous step, into an innovation strategy, aligned with the overall strategy of the firm. The strategy is further required to be complemented by apposite plans. The strategy and plan must have the buy-in and a consistent focus from the senior management.

Driver Requirements

ID 2.1 Innovation Strategy
- The organisation should have an innovation strategy derived from market needs and technology trends.

ID 2.2 Strategic Alignment
- The innovation strategy should be aligned with the overall business strategy of the organisation. This implies that the requirements that emerge from the assessment of *market needs* and *technology trends* should be filtered to consider only those innovation requirements, which are in line with the overall business strategy.

ID 2.3 Innovation Plan

- The organisation should derive an appropriate innovation plan to execute the innovation strategy.
- The plan should at least identify the initiatives, resources, timelines, etc., required for execution.

ID 2.4 Leadership Promotion

- Senior leaders should demonstrate their commitment to innovation. The mode of demonstration maybe through various communications, both verbal and written, and formal and informal, or by any other appropriate means.

ID 2.5 Leadership Review

- Senior leaders should include innovation initiatives in their various reviews.
- The reviews identifies the gaps and provides required support by appropriate means to address the gaps.

Resource Management for Innovation

Judicious management of resources, both human and others, is vital for driving business innovation. Competency identification, development, and provisioning of the resources, etc., are often critical for a successful innovation effort, and intrinsic to the ICaM framework.

Driver Requirements

ID 3.1 Competency Identification
- The organisation should determine the competencies that will help to achieve the requirements as per the innovation strategy (ID2.1) and Plan (ID2.3).

ID 3.2 Human Resources
- The organisation should provide the human resources as per the competencies identified, according to ID3.1.

ID 3.3 Team Empowerment
- The relevant teams driving/supporting innovation should be appropriately empowered to perform their duties. The empowerment should be in the form of decision-making ability

(e.g. piloting a solution, etc.), inclusion in KRAs (Key Result Area), etc.

ID 3.4 Competency Development

- Wherever applicable, the organisation should take appropriate measures to develop competencies, to achieve the requirements as per innovation strategy (ID2.1) and plan (ID2.3).

ID 3.5 Other Resources

- The organisation should identify other resources (e.g., financial, technology, etc.) necessary to achieve the requirements, as per innovation strategy (ID2.1) and plan (ID2.3).

CHAPTER 15

Innovation Process

Kernel of the ICaM framework is the cluster *Innovation Process*. This lays out the critical points to ensure a continuous flow of ideas, and to convert these to profitable business streams. This part has taken cue from Hansen's work as well.[29]

Driver Requirements

Innovation Process

ID 4.1 Idea Sourcing
- The organisation should have a system/process to capture various ideas that may emerge from internal sources and external sources.

ID 4.2 Idea Evaluation
- The organisation should define the criteria to select an idea that might have innovation potential.
- The ideas should be selected for further development, following the defined criteria.

ID 4.3 Product/Service Development
- The organisation should develop the selected ideas into products/ services prototypes.

- The developed prototypes should be tested in a representative controlled group.
- The organisation should provide the resources required for the test (ID3.0).

ID 4.4 Commercialisation

- The product/services should be deployed in the identified market.

CHAPTER 16

Innovation Results

This book views innovation as an idea or invention that generates business results. Innovation, in this perspective, has been defined by the innovation equation:

Innovation = Idea / Invention + Commercialisation + Business Results

Innovation costs resources. Hence, from the perspective of a business firm, it is cardinal that the effort pays in terms of business results i.e. addition to top-line or bottom-line or both. Any innovation effort entails evaluation from this perspective, and product / service that does not yield results need to be discontinued or corrective action taken. The cluster *innovation results* elaborate the process of evaluating an innovation initiative. This work refers to Hansen's (2007)[32] and ADL's (Arthur D Little) (2010)[8] work in the domain.

Driver Requirements

Innovation Process

ID 5.1 Innovation Process Performance
- The following metrics should be tracked to measure the process performance:

o **Idea Generation**– *(a) Number of ideas generated internally, (b) Number of ideas generated externally.*

o **Idea Selection**– *(a) Percentage of ideas selected with respect to total ideas generated.*

o **Idea Development**– *(a) Percentage of ideas funded, compared to total ideas selected, (b) Percentage of funded ideas that generated revenue.*

ID 5.2 Innovation Financial Performance

- The organisation should at least track the following financial metrics from innovation efforts:

  o *Percentage penetration in the desired market*

  o *Revenues from commercialised ideas*

  o *EBIT / cost reduction from commercialised ideas*

  o *Time to break-even / sales volume*

Note on Innovation Financial Performance

Applicability and selection of the metrics

In purview of a new product launch or market entry, it is germane to use all the metrics. However, in certain contexts, specifically in case of a classic process improvement initiative, where sales or market penetration cannot be established, a firm can choose to select the right metric as EBIT or Cost Reduction. In that case, numerical significance of innovation financial performance will be attributed to one metric only.

Linking time to break-even and sales volume

It is cogent at this point to understand the linkage between the time to break-even and sales volume. We shall refer to the following formulae:

Break-even Volume = Fixed Cost / (Price – Variable Cost)

Break-even Period = Break Even Volume / Projected Sales Volume per period

Inferring from this, *sales volume per period* can be referred to for computation, which is an indicative of the time to break-even.

PART 5

Case Contexts – Application of ICaM in XMobile, AllHealthCare, and SmithHan Tools

'It's no use going back to yesterday, because I was a different person then.'

CHAPTER 17

Case Context – Assessment of Innovation Trends

XMobile

Assessment of Market Needs

For assessment of market needs, XMobile has segmented the market geography wise, and further segregation has been done across three product categories, i.e., voice, traditional data, and new hybrid. Market needs pertinent to innovation were determined at this level. The analysis rendered that voice market in the big cities were saturated with penetration more than 150 per cent, thus, leaving scope mostly for process-level innovations or innovation of other new products. Also, as the level of adoption and choices of traditional data and new hybrid products were quite low in small towns, semi-rural, and rural areas, XMobile decided to focus on product innovation in this segment.

Assessment of Technology Trends

XMobile recognises the importance of technology in a telecom industry, and has created a group called Technology Adaptation Research Centre (TARC) within it. While there is no core R & D done by the group,

TARC is expected to keep the stakeholders abreast of relevant technology developments. TARC primarily operates in two domains, network and technology convergence, with the following as focus areas:

- Identify and test technologies – Identify and test technologies in the early adaptation stage that could support XMobile's strategy.
- Application innovation – Evaluation of technologies based on technology life cycle, and work with the architects and business to augment and replace current applications.
- New product development and support – Identify, develop, and test new product opportunities, along with functional users.
- New hybrid – Leverage crowdsourcing to create a network of innovators (Refer chapter 20).

AllHealthCare

Assessment of Market Needs

AllHealthCare closely works with the government and determines the market need based on government vision and industry projections on healthcare. The current focus of Athena government is on rural healthcare. Current revenue contribution of rural is a meagre 12.79 per cent (Fig 8.2) to AllHealthCare's balance sheet. In this perspective, AllHealthCare has planned to concentrate on product innovation, relevant to basic healthcare in rural areas.

Assessment of Technology Trends

Currently, research is not part of the nucleus of AllHealthCare product portfolio and contributes a scanty 2.57 per cent (Fig 8.3) of the revenue. Current government policy is inclined towards basic healthcare and not research. With this in perspective, AllHealthCare does not intend to focus on innovation in this area, and will sustain the current level of performance only.

However, keeping in view the priority of Athena government on rural healthcare, AllHealthCare has set its focus on affordable healthcare technology for rural masses. It has recently signed two agreements – one with a telecom service provider to develop technologies to connect the rural centers, and the second one is with a health technology provider to explore technologies affordable to the rural populace.

SmithHan Tools

Assessment of Market Needs

SmithHan views the market in two segments – hand tool segment and machine tool segment. While there is improvement in the machine tool market, hand tool market is almost matured. Looking at the current trend, SmithHan has decided to focus on process innovation in the hand tool segment to improve efficiency. They have recently initiated a lean management programme to address the efficiency of the processes, with the direct sponsorship from the deputy managing director. The company has also decided to impart a vigorous thrust on product innovation in the machine tool segment to build the top line, and allocated 27 per cent of the budget to drive this.

Assessment of Technology Trends

The core competence of SmithHan is hand tools for the agricultural sector. Boosted by the Athena government incentives on agricultural productivity, SmithHan has decided to realign its focus in the sector, beyond the hand tools segment. With a view to enhance the technological capability, SmithHan has recently signed a contract with an overseas technology provider in the domain. The objective is to explore and create avenues to enhance the scope for the use of machine tools in the agricultural sector.

CHAPTER 18

Case Context – Strategy and Leadership Support

XMobile

Innovation Strategy / Strategy Alignment / Innovation Plan

Strategy of XMobile is driven centrally and the state SBUs (Strategic Business Unit) mostly work on the competitive and operations strategy. The current market strategy of XMobile is centered on three themes:

- Improving the revenue market share through top line growth.
- Enhancement of customer experience through consistent service.
- Product innovation in data and new hybrid to improve the top line.

XMobile has recently started a function to drive innovation. The team operates independently away from the existing operation, in terms of regular financials. The function is headed by a senior person with techno-managerial background, reporting to the technology director. The innovation team works out the innovation strategy, and prepares the relevant innovation plans. This team works very closely with the TARC team (Refer chapter 17).

Leadership Promotion / Leadership Review

The executive council at XMobile comprises the CEO and the functional directors. The innovation focus has been explicitly stated by the executive council, and forms part of a regular review by the council. However, this is yet to become a point of focus in the state's SBUs.

AllHealthCare

Innovation Strategy / Strategy Alignment / Innovation Plan

Based on the assessment of market needs, AllhealthCare has incorporated product innovation as a prime strategic focus. The innovation in AllHealthCare is the responsibility of the health service director, who directly reports to the CEO. There are no specific plans for product innovation, and it is integrated within the overall service plan.

Leadership Promotion / Leadership Review

While the CEO reviews the innovation initiative periodically, it is yet to become part of the grind.

SmithHan Tools

Innovation Strategy / Strategy Alignment / Innovation Plan

SmithHan has always looked at the market needs to decide on the innovation route to be adopted. Based on the market analysis, it has identified product innovation in the agricultural sector as one of its strategic focus. The deputy managing director himself drives this effort and two distinct verticals work with him – a business transformation vertical, to drive the process innovation in the hand tool segment, and an R & D team to work on the machine tool segment. Also, SmithHan has currently introduced plant-level innovation as an initiative across the organisation. Relevant innovation plans and resource allocations are done centrally.

Leadership Promotion / Leadership Review

The corporate level reviews are done from the head office by the deputy managing director. While it is expected at the plant level as well, the right sense, earnest, and rigour are still absent at the site-level reviews.

CHAPTER 19

Case Context – Resource Management for Innovation

XMobile

Competency Identification / Human Resources / Team Empowerment / Competency Development

As part of the overall HR process, XMobile has an integrated structure for competency identification and development, deployed across the organisation. This is linked to the specific skills required for a particular role and there is appropriate focus on skills related to innovation. The innovation unit is empowered to decide on relevant prototypes and piloting away from existing operations.

Other Resources

Any other resources like technology are identified and managed by the innovation team.

AllHealthCare

Competency Identification / Human Resources / Team Empowerment / Competency Development

AllHealthCare's innovation team members are from the service team, who were assessed and proven to have higher analytical abilities. While there is no practice specific competency identification, team members are exposed to various relevant skill development programmes. AllHealthCare has recently taken steps to enhance the innovation team's capability, with the recruitment of a senior healthcare professional, well known in the industry.

Other Resources

Resources, other than human, are as per the service development plan, where innovation constitutes a major part. Most of the other resources identified are high-end medical equipment, to cater to the masses.

SmithHan Tools

Competency Identification / Human Resources / Team Empowerment / Competency Development

SmithHan tool drives innovation at the plant level, and each site is equipped with an innovation specialist reporting to the plant head. Innovation specialists are strong domain specialists in technology, recruited externally or through internal resourcing. There are specific competency needs, mostly technical, identified by the training team.

Other Resources

While the innovation related resources are managed by the deputy managing director himself, plant-level specialists work in tandem with the corporate plan.

CHAPTER 20

Case Context – Innovation Process

XMobile

XMobile has recently launched an automated open innovation platform for capturing ideas that may lead to the development of profitable products. It has focussed specifically on crowdsourcing and has created a network of innovators. The network comprises developers, research institutions, as well as research-focussed universities, which are connected through a web platform. There are well-defined criteria to evaluate a potential idea, and fund it for further piloting. The innovation team carries out the interfacing with the relevant stakeholders. The launch of the platform has visibly improved the percentage of commercially viable ideas.

XMobile has also collaborated with various start-ups in the telecom and other converging domains, to support during the process of idea development to product testing.

AllHealthCare

AllHealthCare is mostly focussed on external resources to generate ideas that can lead to the development of basic services, which is the current focus. They have also developed a web platform connecting health professionals, potential users, and research institutions. AllHealthCare has instituted a reward mechanism to accelerate the rate and quantum of idea generation. The ideas are tested in the current catchment areas, and potential ideas are funded for further development.

Another initiative taken up by AllHealthCare in recent times is the creation of various focus groups. There are age-based groups as well as requirement-based groups. Age-based groups comprise groups like the *Above 60 Club*, or the *Mothers Club* with kids less than five years of age. Requirement based groups are also organised, predicated primarily on diseases.

AllHealthCare periodically organises interactions with the focus groups, to comprehend the requirements. The findings are integrated back to the current service lines or new services are developed.

SmithHan Tools

The business transformation team drives innovations in the hand tool segment, following an in-house methodology, termed as S-I-S; Select – Improve – Sustain. This is driven at the plant level by the innovation specialist for the selected processes. For the machine tool segment, the R & D team works as the pivot, and works in tandem with the potential users as well as technology providers and research institutes. The design philosophy is based on two T's namely, *Test* and *Tick*. SmithHan Tools depends on extensive prototyping, which is commonly referred to as *Test*. The successful prototypes are funded for production, and rolled out in the identified markets. This process has been internally branded as *Tick*. The success rate of Test to Tick is considerably high, benchmarked against similar industries, and is in the range of > 70 per cent.

CHAPTER 21

Case Context – Innovation Results

XMobile

XMobile rigorously tracks the financial performance from the innovation efforts. The results are evaluated against the planned business case or strategic plan. It has defined a scorecard including all the metrics. The scorecard forms a part of the management reviews. Pertinent action is taken, based on the performance of the launched product / service, both before and after the roll out. The launch of the automated platform has directly impacted the level of commercialisation of the inventions across all the defined indices.

AllHealthCare

The current innovation focus of AllHealthCare is on basic healthcare, closely mirroring the government's focus on creating a fundamental spread of basic healthcare. Performances of new products are measured geographically across all relevant indices of ICaM, with special focus on rural areas. Non-performing products are weeded out, looking at the performance in the specific geography. To accelerate rural healthcare in

Athena, AllHealthCare also tracks few other metrics for rural geographies as — *Acceptance of the Product by the rural mass (Indicated by number of people availing it)* and *percentage of people cured.*

SmithHan Tools

SmithHan Tools measures the impact of innovations, both for process innovations and product innovations for the applicable business lines. Benefits of process innovations are tracked at the plant levels and product-related innovations are evaluated centrally. Appropriate actions are taken depending on the results and the addition to either the bottom line (for process innovations) or the top line (product innovations).

PART 6

Assessment and Analysis

'My dear, here we must run as fast as we can, just to stay in place. And if you wish to go anywhere, you must run twice as fast as that.'

CHAPTER 22

Fundamentals of Deploying ICaM

Creating the Baseline

ICaM can be used as the point of reference, as well as an approach to drive innovation. The starting block in deploying ICaM is the creation of a baseline of current performance, pertinent to innovation. This comprises the following building blocks:

- Assessment of the current innovation capability of the firm, using the ICaM framework
- Identification of the innovation drivers on which the firm needs to focus

ICaM Instrument and Criteria

ICaM framework has been converted to an easy-to-use format, termed as *Innovation Capability Assessment Instrument (ICaM Instrument)*. In the instrument, the requirements stated in innovation drivers have been further decomposed into discrete measurable **CRITERIA,** which can be assessed by examining the relevant evidences. Readers may refer to Appendix I for ICaM Instrument.

For example, the assessment of market need has been split into three measurable **CRITERIA** as:

- The organisation has deployed ways and means to know the market needs from customers, in perspective of determining innovation needs and trends appropriate to the organisation.
- The organisation has deployed ways and means to know the market needs from non-customers, in perspective of determining the innovation needs and trends appropriate to the organisation.
- The gained knowledge has been translated to determine the innovation needs that may emerge in the future, which are applicable / appropriate in the context of the organisation.

CHAPTER 23

Assessing and Baselining

Assessing current innovation capability entails determination of the current performance of the innovation drivers. As mentioned in the previous section, for the purpose of assessment, innovation drivers have been split into discrete measurable **CRITERIA.** The axiom is to measure the criteria at a granular and a discretely identifiable level, and roll it up to reflect the current achievement level (see below) of the respective innovation driver.

Assessment Fundamentals

ICaM framework defines two kinds of assessments as depicted in Figure 23.1.

- *Standard Evidence Based Assessment (SEBA)*
- *Complementary Perceptive Assessment (COPA)*

SEBA is the primary measurement. Each driver is determined, based on evidences of deployment available. COPA is where a set of scientifically selected sample of employees across span and layers mark the current performance.

In both the approaches, the ICaM instrument (Appendix I) is used as reference.

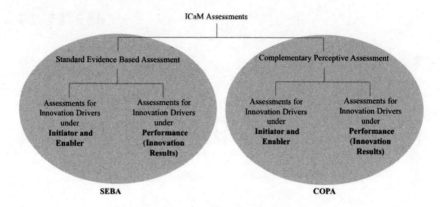

FIGURE 23.1   Assessment Fundamentals

It is important to note that SEBA is the primary and standard approach for assessment of capability across innovation drivers. COPA can be used for cross validation of the findings, compared with organisational perception, and should be used as a complement to SEBA. The context of the use of both the approaches has been illustrated in the following sections.

Defining the Achievement Level for an Innovation Driver

Achievement level is defined as the performance of a firm, measured for an innovation driver (by measuring the criteria) or a metric, as defined below:
    Defining mathematically,

$$\text{Achievement level} = \frac{\text{Score for the innovation driver or the metric}}{\text{Maximum possible score for the driver or the metric}}$$

Following sections elaborate on the assessment and computation of *Achievement Levels* for drivers under *initiator and enabler,* and drivers under *innovation results* for both SEBA and COPA.

SEBA – Assessment for Drivers under Initiator and Enabler

(A) Grading Scale – SEBA

The grading scale in the table below (Table 23.1) is used to measure the level of achievement of various drivers (CRITERIA).

TABLE 23.1 Grading Scale

Level	Extent of Deployment				Description	Score
	Driver (Criteria) Requirement	In How Many units of the Organization	In How Many Areas of the Units	Driven through a structured process		
Fully Implemented (FI)	All	All	All	Driven	Deployment of all requirements in all units in all areas – driven	5–6
Largely Implemented (LI)	Most	Most	Most	Driven	Deployment of most requirements in most units in most areas – driven	4–5
Moderately Implemented (MI)	Many	Many	Many	Driven	Deployment of many requirements in many units in many areas – driven	3–4
Slightly Implemented (SI)	Few	Few	Few	Mostly Discrete, Sometimes Driven	Deployment of many requirements in few units in areas – mostly happening discrete – driven many times	2–3
Discretely Implemented (DI)	Some	Some	Some	Discrete	Deployment of some requirements in some areas – happening discretely	1–2
Not Implemented (NI)	None/ Rare	None/ Rare	None/ Rare	None/ Rare	No evidence of Deployment	0–1

The assessment of a particular driver is on six levels, mentioned as **FI LI MI SI DI NI**. This takes cue from SEI CMM[12] in defining the scale.

It may be noted that, for keeping the assessment simple, rather than selecting the *extent of deployment* across levels, it would be pertinent to select one of the six combinations that reflect the appraised CRITERIA the closest.

In case of cross-level selection of the *extent of deployment*, the score can be decided based on the direction in which most of the scores are inclined. The following guidelines can be referred to for deciding on the score (Numerals below indicate selection at a particular level e.g. 1 – 3 means 1 selection in one level and 3 selections in another level):

- *1 – 3 combination: Score will be according to the level where three selections belong to. E.g., For Many – Some – Some – Discrete, score will be between 1 to 2 (discretely implemented).*
- *1 – 2 – 1 combination: Score will be according to the level where two selections belong to. E.g. For Few – Many – Many – Discrete, score will be between 3 to 4 (moderately implemented).*
- *1 – 1 – 1 – 1 & 2 – 2 combination: It will be apt to look at the evidences.*

(B) Determination of Achievement Level – SEBA

The level of a particular driver (CRITERIA) needs to be determined, based on four dimensions mentioned as *extent of deployment*. The extent of deployment is defined across four dimensions and need to be determined based on the evidences as delineated below. Table 23.1 is required to be used as reference. The four dimensions for extent of deployment are as explained below:

a. **Driver (Criteria) Requirement**
   This signifies the extent of deployment of the CRITERIA of the particular driver.

b. **In how many units of the organisation?**
   If it's a multi-unit / geography firm, it is necessary to assess the *extent of deployment* of the CRITERIA across all units / geographies.

c. **In how many areas of the Unit?**
   Evidences need to be examined in all the functional areas.

d. **Driven through a structured process**
   It is vital to see evidence if there is a structured process to attain a

particular *achievement level* of a certain innovation driver, or if it is just a discrete and ad-hoc occurrence.

(C) Illustrative Computation for Initiator and Enabler – SEBA

The following table (Table 23.2) would be used for illustration. *The computation is shown for two innovation drivers, i.e., assessment of market needs and assessment of technology trends*

Step 1: Collect data inputs (evidences) in column 'D' on the *extent of deployment*. Refer to Table 23.1 above.

Step 2: Decide the scores in Column E'. For example, the first criteria for the *assessment of market needs* is that *the organisation has deployed ways and means to know the market needs from the customer, in perspective of determining innovation needs and trends appropriate to the organisation* (picked up from ICaM instrument in Appendix I).

Assume that for this criterion, the *extent of* deployment is *Most-Most-Most-Driven*. Referring to Table 23.1, the score for this combination is between 4 and 5.

Looking at the evidences, the score awarded here is 4.3.

Step 3: Compute the average score for the CRITERIA, with respect to the innovation driver. Here,

The average Score for:
- *Assessment of Market Need* = [(4.3+2.8+1.9) / 3)] = 3.00
- *Assessment of Technology Trends* = [(5.1+3.2+0.9) / 3)] = 3.07

Step 3: Compute the achievement level for the particular innovation driver using the formula –

[Average Score / Maximum Possible Score] X Numerical Significance of the Driver]

Referring to Figure 11.1, Numerical significance for
- *Assessment of Market Need* = 55
- *Assessment of Technology Trend* = 45

Referring to Table 23.1, the maximum possible Score is always 6.

Here, achievement levels for:
- *Assessment of Market Need* = [(3 / 6)]X 55 = 27.5
- *Assessment of Technology Trends* = [(3.07 / 6)]X 45 = 23.03

TABLE 23.2   Illustrative Computation for Initiator and Enabler – SEBA

(A)	(B)	(C)	(D) Extent of Deployment				(E)	(F)	(G)	(H)
			Driver Require-ment	In How Many Units	In How Many Areas of the Units	Driven through structured Process	Score			
Cluster	Innovation Driver	Criteria					Score	Average Score for Driver	Achievement Level for Driver	Total Score for Cluster
		The organization has deployed ways and means to know the market needs from Customer in perspective of determining Innovation needs and trend appropriate to the organization.	Most	Most	Most	Driven	4.3			
	Assessment of Market Needs	*The organization has deployed ways and means to know the market needs from Non-Customer in perspective of determining Innovation needs and trend appropriate to the organization.*	Few	Few	Few	Mostly Discrete, Sometimes Driven	2.8	3.00	[Average Score (3)/ Possible Score (6) X Numerial Significance of the Driver (55) = 27.5	
		The gained knowledge has been translated to determine the Innovation needs that may emerge in the future which are applicable/apporpriate in the context of the organization.	Some	Some	Some	Discrete	1.9			

Assessment of Innovation Trends						50.53
	The organization deployed was to have a detailed understanding of the emerging Technology Trend appropriate to the organization.	All	All	All	Driven	5.1
Assessment of Technology Trends	*The understanding has led to an assessment of role of Innovation in the competitive positioning.*	Many	Many	Many	Driven	3.2 / 3.07
	The understanding has led to an assessment of the strategic focus required by the organization in perspective of Innovation need.	None/ Rare	None/ Rare	None/ Rare	None/ Rare	0.9

[Average Score 3.07)/ Possible Scorfe (6) X Numerical Significance of the Driver (45) = 23.03

Step 4: Total score for the cluster Assessment of Innovation Trends is computed summing up the score for the constituent drivers.

Here, the score for the cluster is

• *27.5 + 23.03 = 50.53*

Step 5: Convert this to % when it is required to normalise. Here,

• *Assessment of Market Need = 27.5*100/55 = 50%*
• *Assessment of Technology Trends = 23.03 * 100/45 = 51.18%*

SEBA – Assessment for Drivers under Performance (Innovation Results)
(A) Grading Scale – SEBA

Here, innovation results are measured across the metrics defined in Chapter 16. The metrics are measured across two dimensions, as shown

TABLE 23.3   Computation Basics – Process Performance Metrics

Process Performances Metrics	Performance	
	Current Performance (60)	Performance Trend for defined period (100)
No. of ideas generated internally *No. of ideas generated externally* *Percentage of ideas selected with* *respect to total ideas generated* *Percentage of ideas funded* *compared to total ideas selected* *Percentage of funded ideas that* *generated revenue*	Total weight 60 is divided across 5 metrics. Individual metrics performance is computed against target.	Total weight of 100 is divided across 5 metrics. How many times ametric meets the target during the defined time period is computed.

TABLE 23.4   Computation Basics – Financial Performance Metrics

Financial Performances Metrics	Performance	
	Current Performance (60)	Performance Trend for defined period (100)
Percentage penetration in the *desired market* *Revenue from commercialized ideas* *EBIT from commercialized ideas* *Time to Break Even/Sales Volume*	Total weight 100 is divided across 4 metrics. Individual metrics performance is computed against target.	Total weight of 100 is divided across 4 metrics. How many times ametric meets the target during the defined time period is computed.

in the tables above (Table 23.3 & 23.4) for both *innovation process performance* and *innovation financial performance*.

The two dimensions are

• Current Performance
• Performance Trend

For the *innovation financial performance*, a new product launch scenario is considered, where all the metrics are applicable.

(B) Determination of Achievements Levels – SEBA

The tables above depict the measurement in two dimensions – *current performance* and *performance trend*. Computations of achievement levels for both are explained below:

(i) Current Performance

Current performance evinces the performance of a metric for the particular time period (e.g., month) compared against a target. The *current performance* is calculated for the numerical significance assigned to the metric, using the following formula:

Current Performance = [Performance for the current period / Target performance]* Metric Numerical Significance

(ii) Performance Trend

Performance trend signifies performance of the particular metric over a defined period of time.

Performance trend is calculated for the numerical significance, depending on how many times the metric is meeting the target. The following formula is used:

Performance Trend = [No. of times target met / No. of time periods]* Metric Numerical Significance

(C) Illustrative Computation for Innovation Financial Performance – SEBA

The following table (Table 23.5) would be used for illustration. The computation has been shown for only one metric, *i.e., percentage penetration in desired market.*

TABLE 23.5 Illustrative Computation for Innovation Financial Performance – SEBA

Financial Performmance Market	(A) Target (for months)				B1 Current Performance	B2 Current Performance Level of Achivement	C1 Performance Trend				C2 Performance trend Level of Achivement
	M1	M2	M3	M4			M1	M2	M3	M4	
Percentage penetration in the desired market	15	19	25	30	27	[Current Peformance (27)/Target Performance (30)]* Metric Numerical Signifcance (25) – 22.5	18	21	26	27	[No. of times target met (3)/No. of time perios (4)]* Metric Numerical Significance (35) – 26.25

Following is a step-by-step description of the computation.

Step 1: Collect data inputs

- **Target (Column A)** – Collect the period-wise (month wise in this case) targets for the metric. In this case, the total time period is four months indicated as M1, M2, M3 and M4. Targets Market penetration have been decided as shown in the table. Month 4 is the current month.
- **Current Performance (Column B1)** – Collect the performance for the current month. In this case, current month's performance is 27.
- **Performance Trend (Column C1)** – Collect the performance for the considered months. In this case, it is for M1, M2, M3, M4.

Step 2: Compute the achievement levels

- *Current Performance Achievement Level (Column B2)*
  [Performance for the current period (27) / Target performance (30]* Metric Numerical Significance (25) = 22.5
  Metric Numerical Significance is mentioned in Table 23.4
- *Performance Trend Achievement Level (Column C2)*
  [No. of times target met (3) / No. of time periods (4)]* Metric Numerical Significance (35) = 26.25
  Metric Numerical Significance is mentioned in Table 23.4

Step 3: Compute the *innovation financial performance* adding the individual *achievement levels* for the rest of the metrics. We will assume the other values as in the following table (Table 23.6)

TABLE 23.6   Illustrative Metrics – Financial Performance – SEBA

Financial Performance Metrics	Current Performance	Performance Trend
Percentage penetration in the desired market	22.2	26.25
Revenue from commercialized ideas	23	27.5
EBI/Cost Reduction from commercialised ideas	21.5	28
Time to Break Even	24.5	28.5
	91.20	110.25

Innovation financial performance is computed adding achievement levels for all the metrics, with respect to both, the current performance and the performance trend.

Here,

Innovation Financial Performance = 91.20 + 110.25 = 201.45

Step 4: For normalising, this needs to be converted to a scale of 100, compared with the numerical weight for innovation financial performance, i.e. 240.

[Innovation Financial Performance (201.45) / Numerical Significance of Innovation Financial Performance (240)] X 100 = 63.75

COPA – Important points

Perceptive assessment is the simplest of the lot, and it is done by the selected respondents for a particular innovation driver. Following are the critical points while deploying this approach.

Sample Selection

- Sample respondents should be representative of the spans and layers of the company.
- The sample size can be decided, based on any standard statistical method.

Knowledge about ICaM

- The selected respondents should have the knowledge of the ICaM framework.
- An exacting requirement is that the person doing the assessment understands the Grading Scale, as described in Table 23.1 above.
- While the person (sample) is not required to collect evidence for the assessment, it is important that he/she uses knowledge-based judgment and experience together.

Creating a core mass of samples

- It is imperative that a core mass of sample respondents is created over time. While there would be samples exiting and new ones being included, a core mass will cinch variation to a minimum.

COPA – Assessment for Drivers under Initiator and Enabler

(A) Grading Scale – COPA

Grading Scale for COPA is the same as in SEBA, as illustrated in Table 23.1.

(B) Determination of Achievement Level – COPA

The maxims of determination of achievement levels for COPA are same as in SEBA explained above.

(C) Illustrative Computation for Initiator and Enabler – COPA

The following table (Table 23.7) would be used for illustration. The computation is shown for two innovation drivers, i.e., *assessment of market needs and assessment of technology trends*.

Step 1: Select the right samples across the relevant span and layers. Example illustrated here considers six samples.

Step 2: The selected samples fill up column (E), following the grading scale in Table 23.1. It is critical to train the selected samples on the criteria in Table 23.1.

Step 3: Compute the average score for the CRITERIA, with respect to the innovation driver. Here,

The average score for
- *Assessment of Market Need = 4.58*
- *Assessment of Technology Trends = 3.86*

Step 4: Compute achievement level for the particular innovation driver using the formula –

[Average Score / Maximum Possible Score] X Numerical Significance of the driver.

Referring to Table 18.1, Maximum Possible Score is always 6.
Here, achievement levels for
- *Assessment of Market Need = [(4.58 / 6)]X 55 = 41.98*
- *Assessment of Technology Trends = [(3.86 / 6)]X 45 = 28.95*

TABLE 23.7 Illustrative Computation for Initiator and Enabler – COPA

(A) Cluster	(B) Innovation Driver	(C) Criteria	(E) Sample 1	Sample 2	Sample 3	Sample 4	Sample 5	Sample 6	(F) Average Score for Driver	(G) Achievement Level for Driver	(H) Total Score
		The organization has deployed ways and means to know the market needs from Customer in perspective of determining Innovation needs and trend appropriate to the organization.	4.3	4.8	5.4	4.1	3.9	4.9			
	Assessment of Market Needs	*The organization has deployed ways and means to know the market needs from Non-Customer in perspective of determining Innovation needs and trend appropriate to the organization.*	3.5	4.7	3.7	5.4	3.7	3.6	4.58	[Average Score (4.58)/ Possible Score (6)] X Numerical Significance of the Driver (55) = 41.98	
		The gained knowledge has been translated to determine the Innovation needs that may emerge in the future which are applicable/appropriate in the context of the organization.	4.1	5.4	4.4	5.5	6	4.6			
Assessment of Innovation Trends		*The organization deployed was to have*									70.93

Assessment of Technology Trends						[Average Score 3.86]/ Possible Scorfe (6) X Numerical Significance of the Driver (45) = 28.95
a detailed understanding of the emerging Technology Trend appropriate to the organizaton.	5.1	4.5	5.2	5.4	4.8	3.2
The understanding has led to an assessment of role of Innovation in the competitive positioning.	3.2	4.5	5.4	3.8	4.7	3.9
The understanding has led to an assessment guided the strategic focus required by the organization in perspective of Innovation need.	0.9	0.1	1.5	3.4	4.5	5.3

Step 5: Score for the cluster *Assessment of Innovation Trends* is determined adding the scores for the constituent drivers.

Here, cluster score = 41.98 + 28.95 = 70.93

Step 6: Convert this to % when it is required to normalise. Here,

- *Assessment of Market Need = (41.98 X 100)/55 = 76.32 %*
- *Assessment of Technology Trends = (28.95 * 100)/45 = 64.33 %*

COPA – Assessment for Drivers under Performance (Innovation Results)

(A) Grading Scale – COPA

The grading scale for COPA is the same as in SEBA, as illustrated in Table 23.3 and 23.4 (i.e. computation basics).

(B) Determination of Achievement Level – COPA

The maxims of determination of achievement levels for COPA are the same as in SEBA explained above.

However, both *current performance* and *performance trend* are indicated by the selected samples.

(C) Illustrative Computation for Performance (Innovation Results) – COPA

The following table (Table 23.8) would be used for illustration. The computation has been shown for all the metrics for innovation financial performance.

Step 1: Collect data inputs from the selected samples. Here, six samples are shown for illustration:

- *Current performance* in column B
- *Performance trend in* column D

It is to be noted that these are derived numbers by the respondents. The respondents should use the similar approach as in the illustrative computations for SEBA.

Step 2: Compute the *achievement levels,* which are the average for all the samples

TABLE 23.8 Illustrative Computation for Performance (Innovation Results) – COPA

(A) Financial Performance Metrics	(B) Current Performance						(C) Achievement Level	(D) Performance Trend						(E) Achievement Level
	Sample 1	Sample 2	Sample 3	Sample 4	Sample 5	Sample 6		Sample 1	Sample 2	Sample 3	Sample 4	Sample 5	Sample 6	
Performance penetration in the desired market	22.4	24.1	19.8	24.0	23.4	21.0	22.42	21.3	23.2	18.9	23.1	22.5	20.1	21.47
Sales from commercialized ideas	23.0	22.8	21.6	24.4	23.7	24.5	23.33	23.1	22.9	21.7	24.5	23.8	24.6	23.46
EBIT from commercialized ideas	21.6	18.9	25.0	21.5	23.8	24.0	22.47	21.8	19.1	25.2	21.7	24.0	24.2	22.62
Time to Break Even	23.0	25.4	24.0	24.5	24.6	24.9	24.40	22.1	24.5	23.1	23.6	21.7	24.0	23.17
						Total	92.62							90.71

- For *current performance* in column C
- For *performance trend* in column E

Step 3: Calculate the total of *achievement levels* for both, *current performance* and *performance trend,* indicated as Total in the table above.

Step 4: Compute the *innovation financial performance,* adding the totals for *current performance* and *performance trend.*

Here,

Innovation Financial Performance = 92.62 + 90.71 = 183.33

Step 4: For normalising, this needs to be converted to a scale of 100, compared with the Numerical Weight for Innovation Performance, i.e., 240

Innovation Financial Performance (183.33) / Numerical Significance of Innovation Financial Performance (240)] X 100 = 76.39

Which one to use – SEBA or COPA

SEBA is the primary approach for the assessment of innovation capability using ICaM. It is important to acknowledge that SEBA is dependent on evidences, with an intrinsic ability to reflect the exactness on ground.

COPA is a complementary approach and can support SEBA to cross-validate findings.

Both the approaches need to be used in tandem, and one can identify two stages from the perspective of time and usage:

- During the initial stage of deployment of ICaM, a firm should depend only on SEBA. COPA should be used to complement the result. Few instances of analysing both synchronously are presented in Chapter 25.
- Once the organisation matures in its innovation capability, it can gradually opt to start using COPA. The advantages of the use of COPA is less turnaround time required and lower cost. However, the quality of findings will depend on the extent of variation amongst the respondents, and with the on-ground reality. The degree of variation is also affected by the stability of the core mass of the samples as mentioned above.

CHAPTER 24

Expressing Results and Analysis

The previous chapter lays down the assessment of the *achievement levels* of the innovation drivers. Cryptic clues contained in this data require to be converted into meaningful information. The next stage involves expressing the data in coherent measures, to derive executable decisions.

Types of Analysis

Following table (Table 24.1) is an illustrative summary of various measures for expressing the data.

It is necessary to note that this doesn't represent an exclusive list of possible assessments and analysis, and readers are welcome to use any other appropriate assessment / tool to arrive at business-relevant decisions.

Each type of assessment is divided into categories based on the mathematical / statistical complexities, involved in the computation.

Basic Assessments

Basic assessment involves simple and easy-to-use mathematical operations.

TABLE 24.1   Types of Analysis

Types of Assessment	Basic Assessment	Advanced Assessment
(A) Innovation Capability Assessment	(1) Index Level Assessment (2) Driver Level Assessment (3) Innovation Capability Profiling	
(B) Innovation Capability Trend Analysis	(1) Metrics Level Trend (2) Driver Level Trend	
(C) Agreement/Variation Analysis	(1) Driver Level Variation	(2) Variation amongst respondents in COPA and/with SEBA
(D) Configuration and Thresholds		(1) Configurations Thresholds

Advanced Assessments

Advanced Assessments use various statistical models, and may require the use of appropriate statistical software, such as Minitab[49] or SPSS. This book uses **Minitab** for all advanced assessments.

Individual assessments are explained in the following section:

(A) Innovation Capability Analysis

INDEX LEVEL ASSESSMENT

Index level assessment provides a snapshot of innovation capability of an organisation, with the help of defined metrics at an aggregate level.

Indices can be determined by using data collected by both the methods, SEBA and COPA.

The following indices have been defined for index level assessment.

Initiating Innovation Capability Index (IICI)

This metric is the aggregate of *achievement levels* across *assessment of innovation trends*. IICI indicates the capability of the organisation to assess *market needs* and *technology trends*, and convert to innovation needs.

Enabling Innovation Capability Index (EICI)

Aggregate *achievement levels* of innovation drivers across *innovation strategy and leadership, resource management for innovation,* and *innovation process,* are expressed as *enabling innovation capability index.* The capability of the organisation to manage internal drivers of innovation is specified by this metric.

Performance Innovation Capability Index (PICI)

PICI is aggregate *achievement levels* across performance indices, both for *innovation process performance* and *innovation financial performance.* The metric indicates effectiveness of the result of the innovation initiatives – both from a perspective of innovation processes and effectiveness of commercialisation.

Overall Innovation Capability Index (OICI)

OICI is the sum total of achievement levels across all innovation drivers and signifies the overall innovation capability.

Referring to Figure 11.1, maximum possible Numerical Significance of the indices are –

- IICZ – 100
- EICI – 500
- PICI – 400
- OICI – 1000

All the metrics can be expressed in percentages for normalisation.

DRIVER LEVEL ASSESSMENT

The current performance of an innovation driver is expressed in driver level assessment. Driver level assessment is critical and can be used to decide on the innovation driver entailing focus.

A common form of driver level assessment is a bar diagram of *achievement levels* for each of the innovation drivers. The performance can be expressed in percentage for normalisation purposes.

Driver level assessment can be performed for both SEBA and COPA.

INNOVATION CAPABILITY PROFILING

Innovation capability profiling is an aggregate level analysis. The plot indicates the areas where a firm needs to focus on to drive innovation.

In this plot, standard deviations are plotted across X and *achievement levels* of the innovation drivers are plotted across the Y axis for all 18 innovation drivers.

The plotted area is divided into three zones to help organisations decide where to deploy resources to drive innovation, depending on the average score and standard deviation. The zones are demarcated as:

- **Sustain**: *Low Variation – High Average*
- **Focus** *– Low Variation – Low Average* and
- **Revisit** *– High Variation – High/Low Average.*

Readers may appreciate that, innovation capability profiling is more appropriate for COPA, where one can easily evaluate the standard deviation amongst the respondents. For using this in case of SEBA, few rounds of measurement will be necessary.

(B) Innovation Capability Trend Analysis

Trend analysis is a plot of *achievement levels* on a time scale. The plot can manifest the performance for a defined period of time. Trend analysis can be used for both SEBA and COPA. Data used can be in absolute values or in percentage.

Referring to Table 24.1, trend analysis can be carried out at both, metric and innovation driver level.

(C) Agreement / Variation Analysis

Driver Level Variation

Variation of the *achievement levels* of SEBA and COPA assessment for each innovation driver is computed.

The variation indicates the ability of the model to reflect the ground reality, as assessed by the respondents.

Variation amongst respondents in COPA and / with SEBA

Variations 'amongst the respondents' and variation of 'respondents and the standard assessments' are determined. Attribute Agreement Analysis[*] is used for the assessment.

(D) Configurations and Thresholds

CONFIGURATIONS

Various cluster level configurations, conducive to innovation, are determined using the *Best Subset Regression** technique. Configuration analysis can be helpful in deciding on the optimum combination of the innovation drivers to enhance innovation capability.

THRESHOLDS

In this, thresholds of the clusters that would maximise the level of innovation is determined using the *Response Optimisation** technique. This can be used to decide the extent of the relative focus on a particular cluster.

For all these three analyses – Attribute Agreement Analysis, Best Subset Regression and Response Optimization, this book uses Minitab for computations.

The next chapter illustrates the analyses with reference to the case of XMobile.

Attribute Agreement Analysis – Examines the agreement of nominal or ordinal ratings. *Best Subset Regression* – Identifies models with less no. of predictors, compared with the full model; *Response Optimisation* – Determines the level of input settings to optimise response(s)

CHAPTER 25

Illustrative Results

The previous section is an annotation of how the results can be represented for arriving at executable business decisions.

This section is an illustration of real-life application of ICaM framework, and depicts how the results are expressed and interpreted. We have considered the case of XMobile.

(A) Innovation Capability Assessment

Index Level Assessment

Following table (Table 25.1) is the assessment of innovation capability at metrics levels.

TABLE 25.1   Index Level Assessment

	Innovation Capability Indices*	Maximum Possible *Numerical Significance*	*Achievement Level* from SEBA	*Achievement Level from COPA*
	(A)	(B)	(C)	(D)
XMobile	OICI	1000	41.6	39.2
	IICI	100	41.0	55.0
	EICI	500	42.8	48.8
	PICI	400	40.3	23.25

The columns in the result tables are

- Column A – Indices as mentioned in index level assessment in Chapter 24
- Column B – Numerical significance for the particular index (Refer chapter 24)
- Column C – *Expresses* the *achievement level (in %)* from SEBA
- Column D – *Expresses* the *achievement level (in %)* from COPA

The shaded cells indicate the area where XMobile is not doing well and needs focus. As shown in the table, *performance innovation capability* requires focus, as compared to the other indices.

However, this data needs to be interpreted in conjunction with the innovation capability profiling and agreement/variation analysis presented below, to take cognizance of the sources of variation.

Driver Level Assessment

The following diagram (Figure 25.1) shows a driver level assessment depicted in a bar diagram

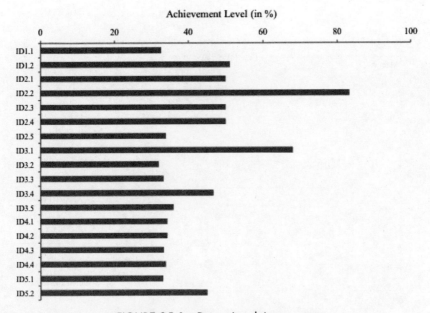

FIGURE 25.1   Driver Level Assessment

From this, the organisation can decide on the innovation drivers to be focussed on. The driver to focus can be decided, predicated on the criteria as:

- *Bottom three Drivers,*
- *Comparing with average,*
- *Comparing with median, etc.*

Innovation Capability Profiling

Standard Deviation and *Achievement Level in* percentage across X and Y axis have been plotted for all 18 innovation drivers, and is shown below (Figure 25.12) for all three cases.

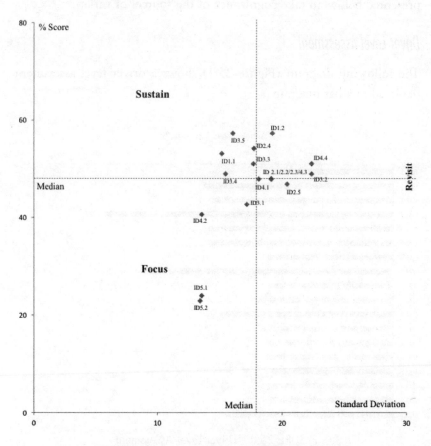

FIGURE 25.2   Innovation Capability Profiling

As mentioned in the previous chapter, the area has been divided into three zones to help organisations to decide where to deploy resources to drive innovation, depending on the average score and standard deviation. The zones are demarcated as:

- **Sustain**: *Low Variation – High Average*
- **Focus:** *Low Variation – Low Average* and
- **Revisit:** *High Variation – High/Low Average.*

(B) Innovation Capability Trend Analysis

Following (Figure 25.3) is a representative innovation capability trend analysis for XMobile. The absolute values of *achievement levels* in time duration of a quarter have been used in the diagram.

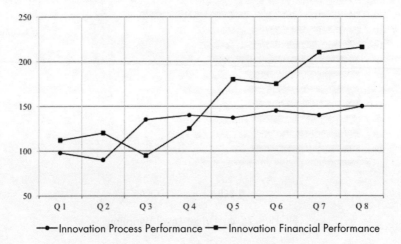

FIGURE 25.3   Innovation Capability Trend Analysis

An improving trend can be observed from quarter three, both for innovation process performance and innovation financial performance. Intrinsically, innovation financial performance is directly proportionate to the innovation process performance, which is visible distinctly in the depiction. Innovation process performance here is due to the launch of the automated crowdsourcing platform by XMobile.

Sustained improving trend affirms the need to continue the initiatives in the area of managing innovation process.

(C) Agreement / Variation Analysis
Driver Level Variation

Following (Figure 25.4) is an analysis of the variation of the respondents, with the standard assessment to distinguish the sources of variation across all drivers.

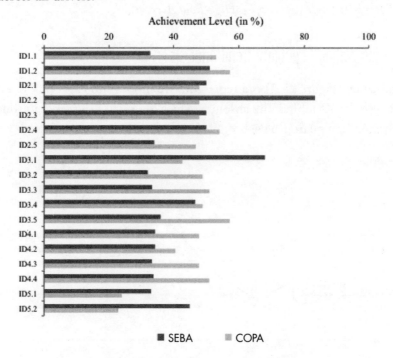

FIGURE 25.4   Driver Level Variation

For most of the innovation drivers, the assessment by the respondents is higher, compared with the standard assessment. This is symptomatic of the difference in perception of innovation amongst employees at different levels. From an organisational action perspective, this illustrates the specific areas where further focus is required to drive innovation.

Variation amongst respondents in COPA and / with SEBA

The summary of agreement analysis is as shown in the table below (Table 25.2) for all three cases:

TABLE 25.2 Variation amongst respondents in COPA and / with SEBA

Agreement Amongst Respondents in COPA			Agreement of Respondents (COPA) with SEBA		
95% Confidence Interval	Kendall's Coefficient	Fleiss Kappa	95% Confidence Interval	Kendall's Coefficient	Fleiss Kappa
(0.00, 15.33)	33.67%	0.049	(0.00, 15.33)	19.15%	0.162

The confidence interval is the range of agreement expected with a 95 percent confidence level. ***Kendall's Coefficient*** signifies the degree of association, and a higher score is better. ***Fleiss Kappa*** denotes the strength of agreement, and can range from −1 to 1; the more the value is away from zero, stronger is the association. The portrayal demonstrates a low / medium range of agreement amongst the respondents, as well as with the standard; an obvious indicator of low degree of understanding of innovation performance in XMobile.

(D) Configurations and Thresholds

Configurations

Table 25.3 ferrets out the various configurations of the innovation drivers at the cluster level conducive to innovation, which can be used by an organisation to optimise the resources deployed for innovation. The best Subset Regression method has been used for the analysis and illustration for two cases. Minitab has been used for the analysis.

Each line in the table represents a model. Var indicates the number of predictors in the model. R_{sq} is the quantum of variation, explained by the predictors. Mallows C_p defines precision-less is the value of C_p, more precise the model is. For each combination of the predictors, the best model has been indicated by the shading. As observed, five predictors model is the obvious combination, accounting for the best Rsq value, and the lowest C_p value. The second best combination is the four predictor model. The higher predictor model evinces the need for a uniform focus across clusters.

TABLE 25.3   Innovation Conducive Configurations – Cluster Level

	Vars	Rsq	Mallow Cp	Cluster 1	2	3	4	5
	1	68.8	144587.1			X		
	1	66.4	155386.1		X			
	1	53.1	217135.5	X				
	2	93.8	28467			X		X
	2	89.1	50404.2		X			X
	2	85.1	69138.9	X				X
Case 1	3	97.6	11251.4		X		X	X
	3	96.9	14181.9		X	X		X
	3	95.6	20136			X	X	X
	4	99.5	2149.9		X	X	X	X
	4	99.5	2258.5	X	X		X	X
	4	97.4	12028.2	X		X	X	X
	5	100	6	X	X	X	X	X

Thresholds

This analysis uses a five predictor model to decide the range of thresholds for the clusters, to achieve an optimum level. Here, we have considered

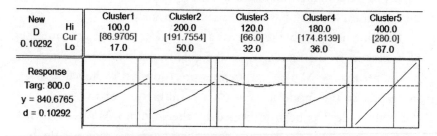

FIGURE 25.5   Cluster-level Thresholds

* For cluster definition,refer to table 11.1.

a level of 800. Response optimisation has been used for the analysis. The output is as given in Figure 25.5. Minitab has been used for the analysis.

The optimum thresholds are indicated by the middle top line denoted as "Cur" which is the current value. The numbers are indicative, and this analysis can be used to decide on the proportion of resources and focus that need to be directed towards the respective cluster.

PART 7

Conclusion

'You're thinking about something, my dear, and that makes you forget
to talk. I can't tell you just now what the moral of that is, but I shall
remember it in a bit.'
'Perhaps it hasn't one', Alice ventured to remark.
'Tut, tut, child!' said the Duchess. 'Everything's got a moral, if only you
can find it.'

CHAPTER 26

A Recipe for the CEO

From Aesop's Fables: The Fox and the Cat

One of the Aesop's Fables narrates the story about a contemptuous fox and a worldly cat.

During one of his sojourns to the neighborhood jungle, the cat happened to meet this fox, who was known for his artful exploits in many skills.

They exchanged pleasantries when they first met at a crossroad in the jungle, under the big banyan tree. They conversed for some time on the current scenario and challenges of living in the jungle, when the fox started swaying to boast of his clout. 'You know', the fox said, 'I have mastered a few hundred problem-solving techniques. No matter what the danger is, I have a solution to come out of the problem'. 'And', he continued, 'I have done this many times'. The cat was abashed, because he did not possess any of the fox's skills. He mewed, 'I am really feeling demeaned in front of you, the great fox ... the only skill I have mastered is to climb trees'.

The fox burst out in laughter. At the same time, there was a clamour from the direction of the nearby village. It was the sound of a pack of dogs from the village barking and galloping furiously at them. There was no time to think, except to save their lives.

The fox was at his wit's end now. He was baffled at which one of his masteries he should use in this situation. However, the cat was very clear and started climbing up the big banyan tree and perched safely on a trunk high above the ground. While he was watching the happenings, the fox was still confused and was not able to judge the best technique to resort to. He was thinking and thinking, while the dogs were still charging briskly at him with vengeance. It was now becoming too late for the fox; the doom was nearing with force. The dogs now charged together and bucked on the fox in no time, and gleefully earned the best prey of the day.

ICaM and 'Fox Dilemma' in driving Innovation

As evinced in the previous section, including the cases of Apple, 3M, and Google, unless equipped with a structured approach, the woe of driving innovation in a firm more often than not, starts right here. The 'Fox Dilemma' of being confused with too many options surfaces every time one contrives an initiative on innovation.

ICaM, as clear from the enumerations and illustrations in the previous chapter, can act as an ameliorative for a business manager to drive innovation in a firm, following a pragmatic and structured approach with the use of optimum resources.

CHAPTER 27

Recommendations

Recommendations for Use

The strength of the ICaM lies in the fact that, it is a double-edged framework. This connotes that while it is built on evidence-based measurement, one can use the same to assess the organisation's perception on innovation as well. The following few points are suggested while using the framework:

- Organisations can deploy the framework as a whole, or just few relevant parts. For example, an organisation could decide to deploy only 'assessment of innovation trends', or the 'innovation process' or just decide to assess 'innovation results'.
- Organisations should adopt the evidence-based measurement to assess the level of a specific driver. It could be substantiated with a carefully selected sample across spans and layers.
- Assessment of innovation results is very critical to the success of deployment.

Is ICaM the perfect framework to drive innovation?

The framework has been tested in few organisations across industry sectors, and has proved to be substantially industry agnostic. Strength of the framework also lies in the facts that, a firm can choose to use the framework in parts or as a whole. The author doesn't claim this to be the perfect panacea – further research can definitely fine-tune the model. However, for an organisation to drive innovation, the framework is pragmatic enough to create a linkage with business strategy, as well as to assure business results.

Lastly ....

Innovation is complex and putting it within a structured ambit is always challenging. While a framework like this provides generic guidance to help an organisation to become innovative by focussing on the right ingredients, it further entails consistent effort, smart work, and being creative beyond a defined boundary. This is similar to cooking with a recipe – while many people can follow the same recipe, the taste is never the same.

Probably, the following incident about Edison described by MA Rosanoff summarises the context of innovation quite well.[66]

I approached him in a humble spirit: 'Mr. Edison, please tell me what laboratory rules you want me to observe.' And right then and there, I got my first surprise.

He spat in the middle of the floor and yelled out:

Hell! there ain't no rules around here! We are tryin' to accomplish somep'n!'
And he walked off, leaving me flabbergasted.

With the Master . . . .

Disciple: Then what is ICaM, master?

Master: What do 'you' envisage my son?

Disciple: Master, is it not the Holy Grail – the Holy Grail of innovation?

Master: Beautiful thought…are you sure my son? I am not…!

Disciple: Then, what is ICaM, master?

Master: Is it the Holy Grail of innovation?…. I don't know my son…
…but I deem, it contains the codes…the arcane codes to guide you in the
successful quest of innovation.

ICaM Instrument

Instructions

Please refer to Chapter 23: Assessing and Baselining

Sl. No.	Driver	Description	Rating
1	**Assessment of Market Technology**	The organisation has deployed ways and means to know the market needs from Customers in perspective of determining Innovation needs and trends appropriate to the organisation.	
		The organisation has deployed ways and means to know the market needs from Non-Customers in perspective of determining Innovation needs and trends appropriate to the organisation.	
		The gained knowledge has been translated to determine the Innovation needs that may emerge in the future which are applicable/appropriate in the context of the organisation.	
2	**Assessment of Technology Trends**	The organisation deployed ways to have a detailed understanding of the emerging Technology Trends appropriate to the organisation.	
		The understanding has led to an assessment of role of Innovation in the competitive positioning.	

Sl. No.	Driver	Description	Rating
		The understanding has led to an assessment that guided the strategic focus required by the organisation in perspective of Innovation needs.	
3	Innovation Strategy	The organisation has an Innovation strategy derived from the Assessment of Market Need and Technology Trends.	
4	Strategic Alignment	The Innovation Strategy is in line with the overall Business Strategy of the organisation.	
5	Innovation Plan	There are Innovation Plans appropriate to the organisation derived from the Innovation Strategy. The Innovation Plan identifies at least the Initiatives, Resources, Timelines etc. required for execution.	
6	Leadership Promotion	The Senior Leaders demonstrate commitment to Innovation by appropriate means.	
7	Leadership Review	The Innovation Initiatives are part of review by Senior Leaders. Reviews identify the gaps and provides required support to address the gaps.	
8	Competency Identification	The organisation has determiend the compet-encies that will help to achieve the requirements as per the Innovation Strategy and Plan.	
9	Human Resources	The organisation has provided the human resources as per the competencies identified.	
10	Team Empowerment	The relevant teams driving/supporting Innovation have been appropriately empowered to perform their duties (e.g. inclusion in Key Result Areas etc.).	
11	Competency Development	The organisation has been taking measures to develop competencies to achieve the require-ments as per Innovation Strategy wherever applicable.	
12	Other Resources	The organisation has identified other resources (e.g. Financial, Technological etc.) required to	

Sl. No.	Driver	Description	Rating
		achieve the requirements as per Innovation Strategy and Plan.	
		The organisation provides the identified resources.	
13	Idea Sourcing	The organisation has a system/process to capture various ideas that may emerge from Internal Sources.	
		The organisation has a system/process to capture various ideas that may emerge from External Sources.	
14	Idea Evaluation	The organisation has defined the criteria to select ideas that might have an Innovation potential to commercialize.	
		The ideas are selected for further development following the defined criteria.	
15	Product/ Service Development	The selected ideas are developed to products/ services prototypes.	
		The developed prototypes are tested in a representative controlled group.	
		The organisation provides the resources required for the test.	
16	Commercia-lisation	The viable ideas have been commercialised.	
17	Innovation Process Performance	No. of ideas generated internally.	
		No. of ideas generated externally.	
		Percentage of ideas selected with respect to total ideas generated.	
		Percentage of ideas funded compared to total ideas selected.	
		Percentage of funded ideas that generated revenue.	
18	Innovation Financial Performance	Percentage penetration in the desired market.	
		Sales from commercialised ideas.	
		EBIT from commercialised ideas.	
		Time to Break Even.	

Discussion Questions

Chapter 10

1) Discuss various definitions of innovation from an industry applicability perspective. You may refer to definitions beyond this book.

2) Referring to the innovation equation, should the terms have different significance? Take examples from various industries and examine.

3) Can the innovation equation be applied in case of a social organisation? Discuss how.

4) How can innovation be viewed as a system-building activity? Illustrate with industry examples.

5) Choose an industry and illustrate the terms *Radical Innovation* and *Incremental Innovation* with relevant examples.

6) Amongst the three perspectives of innovation (market / industry, value chain, product life cycle), which one is more important from the perspective of an organisation? Discuss referring examples of companies from different industries.

7) Take the example of a common product and analyse the S-Curve for it. What might be a technological discontinuity for it (Hint – You can take example of TV / car etc.)?

8) Assess Transilience Map from the point of view of practical application. Select an example of innovation for a company and detail out the managerial and technical traits required for dominating the market place?

9) Can an existing innovation be disrupted due to regulation? Examine with the help of an appropriate example.

10) How important is the role of people in innovation, compared with that of technology? Analyse with examples.

11) Work out the specifications for an open innovation system for a select company (hint – use Table 10.1).

12) Why is it important to measure innovation capability? Illustrate.

Chapter 11 to 16

1) Referring to ICaM framework, should the numerical significance of the innovation drivers vary depending on the industry? Explain with examples (Hint – For example, should the *Numerical Significance* for *Assessment of Technological Trend* vary for a telecom company from that of a FMCG company?).

2) Referring to *innovation results* in ICaM framework, what is your view on a company choosing its own metrics, rather than deploying the metrics defined in the ICaM framework? Can you think of some alternate metrics for both process and financial performance? You may take examples of a specific company and innovation.

Chapter 22 to 25

1) Analyse to list a few more approaches for expressing results and analysis of findings from the deployment of ICaM

Case Application

Select a company and create a baseline using ICaM. Apply both SEBA and COPA approaches.

Deliverables

1. Create a baseline referring to Chapter 24 & 25. Apart from the approaches illustrated in the book to express results, you may select any other appropriate method / tool.
2. Create descriptive analytical notes for each of the innovation drivers. Please refer to the results of baseline from the previous step. The analytical notes should at least contain
   a. Current status
   b. Areas to focus
   c. Action plan
3. Create a presentation to the senior management, emphasising on:
   a. Current performance,
   b. Improvement areas and
   c. Action plan

Hints – SEBA

- Agree with senior management for the exercise
- Create a team for assessment using SEBA
- Brief / train the team
- Calibrate the team with small pilot
- Create the baseline performance

Hints – COPA

- Select the right size of respondents
- Rests of the actions are same as SEBA

Hints – Senior Management Presentation

- This is a presentation to the senior management. You may like to include:
  o Executive summary of 2 / 3 pages illustrating findings, gaps, and action plans
  o Detailed analysis

References

1. 3M Company (2002): A Century of Innovation – The 3M Story: Company Publication, Minnesota, p. 30.
2. Abernathy William J and Clark Kim B (1985): Innovation – Mapping the Winds of creative destruction: Elsevier Science Publishers B.V.
3. Adner Ron (2006): Match your Innovation strategy to Innovation Ecosystem: Apr 2006.
4. Afuah A (2003): *Innovation Management – Strategies Implementation and Profits*: Oxford University Press, Oxford, p. 117.
5. Afuah A (2003): *Innovation Management – Strategies Implementation and Profits*: Oxford University Press, Oxford, p. 13.
6. Afuah A (2003): *Innovation Management – Strategies Implementation and Profits*: Oxford University Press, Oxford, p. 37.
7. Anthony Scott D (2012): The Little Black Book of Innovation: Harvard Business School Publishing Corporation, Boston, p. 72.
8. Arthur D Little (2010): *Pathways to Innovation Excellence*: Arthur D Little, 2010.
9. Ashiho LS (2003): Mobile Technology – Evolution from 1G to 4G: Electronics for You, June, 2003.
10. Booz & Co (2010): *The Global Innovation 1000 – How the Top Innovators keep Winning*: Booz & Co, 2011.
11. Carnegie Mellon University (2010): *CMMI for Development Version 1.3*: Nov 2010, p. 39.

12. Carnegie Mellon University (2011): Standard CMMI Appraisal Method for Process Improvement (SCAMPI) A, Version 1.3: Method Definition Document: Mar 2011.

13. Chesbrough Henry (2006): Open Innovation: Harvard Business School Publishing Corporation, Boston, p. XXIV.

14. Chesbrough Henry (2006): Open Innovation: Harvard Business School Publishing Corporation, Boston, XVII.

15. Christensen M Clayton (2004): The Innovators Dillema: Harvard Business School Press, New York, p. XVIII.

16. COPC (2012): *COPC CSP Standard*: May 2012, p. 49.

17. Dalal, Sanjay (2012): Apple's Innovation Strategy – Learn How Apple and Steve Jobs Innovate (Apple Innovation): KIindle Edition.

18. Dyer Jeff, Gregersen Hal, Christensen Clayton M (2011): *Innovators DNA*: Harvard Business Review Press, Boston, p. 41–153.

19. Essmann H, Preez N. du (2009): *An Innovation Capability Maturity Model – Development and Initial Application*: World Academy of Science Engineering and Technology 53, 2009, 435–446.

20. Executive Office of the President of the United States (2008): University Private Sector Research Parternship in the Innovation Ecosystem, p. 21.

21. Geroski Paul (2003): *The Evolution of New Markets*: Oxford University Press, Oxford, p. 111.

22. Geroski Paul (2003): *The Evolution of New Markets*: Oxford University Press, Oxford, p. 150.

23. Govindarajan Vijay, Trimble Chris (2007): 10 rules for Strategic Innovators – From Idea to Execution: Harvard Business School Press, Boston, p. 185.

24. Govindarajan Vijay, Trimble Chris (2010): The Other Side of Innovation: Harvard Business School Press, Boston, p. 15.

25. Govindarajan Vijay, Trimble Chris (2010): The Other Side of Innovation: Harvard Business School Press, Boston, p. 52.

26. Grossman David (2014): Secret Goodle Lab 'rewards staff for failure': BBC News Technology.

27. Gundling, Ernest (2000): The 3M Way of Innovation – Balancing People and Profits: Kadansha International, Tokyo, p. 15.

28. Gundling, Ernest (2000): The 3M Way of Innovation – Balancing People and Profits: Kadansha International, Tokyo, p. 18.

29. Gundling, Ernest (2000): The 3M Way of Innovation – Balancing People and Profits: Kadansha International, Tokyo, p. 79.

30. Gupta Praveen (2010): *Business Innovation Maturity Model*: www. realinnovation.com, Mar 2010.

31. Hamel G (2006): The Why, What, and How of Management Innovation: Harvard Business Review, Feb 2006.

32. Hansen, T Morten and Birkinshaw Julian (2007): *The Innovation Value Chain*: Harvard Business Review, June 2007, 121–131.

33. http://courses.unt.edu/kt3650_9/sld001.htm.

34. http://en.wikipedia.org/wiki/S_Curve.

35. http://en.wikipedia.org/wiki/Technology_life_cycle.

36. http://www.businessinsider.in/WhatsApp-Is-Growing-Even-Faster-Than-Facebook-Did-When-Facebook-Was-The-Same-Age/articleshow/30699390.cms.

37. http://www.forbes.com/sites/haydnshaughnessy/2013/03/07/who-has-the-winning-innovation-model-google-apple-or-samsung/

38. http://www.greekmythology.com/Myths/Heroes/Perseus/perseus.html.

39. http://www.mooreslaw.org/

40. http://www.wired.com/techbiz/media/news/1998/01/9858.

41. Huston Larry and Sakkab Nabil (2006): Connect and Develop – Inside Procter and Gamble's New Model for Innovation: Harvard Business Review, Mar 2006.

42. Isaacson Walter (2011): *Steve Jobs*: Little Brown, London, p. 464.

43. Jackson Deborah J (2006): What is an Innovation Ecosystem: National Science Foundation, Arlington, VA.

44. Kotler Philip (1983): Principles of Marketing Management:P Prenticew Hall Inc, N J, p. 298, 304.

45. KPMG (2013): *The Mobile Evolution – The challenge and opportunities of mobile*: KPMG International Cooperative, 2013.

46. Leifer R, McDermott Christopher M, O'Connor Gina Colarelli, Peters Lois S, Rice Mark, Veryzer Robert W (1994): Radical Innovation: Harvard Business School Press, Boston, p. 15.

47. Leifer R, McDermott Christopher M, O'Connor Gina Colarelli, Peters Lois S, Rice Mark, Veryzer Robert W (1994): Radical Innovation: Harvard Business School Press, Boston, p. 15.

48. Loren Julian Ketih (2011): A guide to Open Innovation and Crowdsourcing: Kogan Page Ltd., Philadelphia, p. 9.

49. Minitab Inc (2004): *Minitab Release 14-Statistical Software*: Minitab Inc, Pennsylvania, Help.

50. Miyashita Yoko (2012): Evolution of Mobile Handsets and The Impact of Smartphones: InfoCom Research Inc.

51. Moore Geoffrey A (2008): *Dealing with Darwin: How Great Companies Innovate at Every Phase of Their Evolution*: Penguin Group, New York, p. 61.

52. Moore Geoffrey A (2008): *Dealing with Darwin: How Great Companies Innovate at Every Phase of Their Evolution*: Penguin Group, New York, p. 202.

53. NIST (2012): *Baldridge Criteria for Performance Excellence 2011–12*: p. 72.

54. OECD (2005): *OSLO Manual-Guidelines for Collecting and Interpreting Innovation Data*: OECD, OSLO, p. 46.

55. Porter M E (1990): *The Competitive Advantage of Nations*: Free Press, New YOrk, p. 780.

56. Porter, Michael E (1985): Competitive Advantage: The Free Press, New York, p. 11–15.

57. Prothmann, Tobias Muller and Stein, Andre (2011): *FMM – Integrated Innovation Maturity Model of Lean Assessment of Innovation Capability*: XXII ISPIM Conference, June 2011, 1–11.

58. Seidel, Victor P (2012): Open Innovation: University of Oxford Diploma in and Strategy and Innovation, Apr 2012.

59. Tushman Michael L and Rosenkopf Lori (1992): Organizational Determinants of Technological Change – Towards a sociology of technological evolution: Research in Organizational Behaviour, Vol. 14, p. 311–347.

60. Ventresca Marc J (2012): *How Markets Get Built-Institutions, Networks and System Builders (Excerpt from Santos and Eisenhardt, 2009 – Boundary Strategies for Nascent Market: Claim, Democrate, Control)*: University of Oxford Diploma in Strategy and Innovation, Apr 2012.

61. Ventresca Marc J (2012): *Evolution of Markets-TMO in Action (Evidence from Large Technology Systems)*: University of Oxford Diploma in Strategy and Innovation, Apr 2012.

62. Ventresca Marc J (2011): http://www.youtube.com/watch?v=19T3diyqRPg.

63. Wojcicki Susan (2011): The Eight Pillars of Innovation: Google Think Insights.

64. http://en.wikipedia.org/wiki/Steve_Jobs.

65. http://www.innovationmain.com/Apple-eBook.html.

66. www.quoteinvestigator.com/2012/04/19/edison-no-rules/).

Acknowledgement

If anything reflects the creation of the book *Monetising Innovation* best, it is the story of Santiago, the protagonist of the book Alchemist by Paulo Coelho. If any thought echoes it better, it is this quote from the same book, "And, when you want something, all the universe conspires in helping you to achieve it". Santiago, a shepherd from Andalusia has a recurring prophetic dream of a hidden treasure in the land of Egypt. Encouraged by a mysterious man Melchizedek, king of Salem to pursue the dream, Santiago sets off on his journey. He sails across continents, travels through mysterious terrains; encounters unsurmountable barriers, but help always comes along and even unknowns become his friends, unanticipated; helping him to discover what he set out to find.

Monetising Innovation has also been a similar journey; one spread across continents and supported by many. A research oriented book of this kind entails a network of supporting entities and it was there; there has been help, support and propellants which have acted as unseen, gentle forces guiding to the goal……

Dr. Marc J Ventresca, University of Oxford, a doyen in the field of Innovation, my mentor and guide. You have been the motivation for me to take forward the idea of developing the ICaM framework to a pragmatic application. Notwithstanding an ever-occupied schedule, you have reviewed and guided the book to tend to precision. The foreword from you has created the right context where the book is positioned and made it a complete account in the domain. I just want to say, without you, the book would not have become a reality.

Dr. Vijay Govindrajan, Leading Global Management Guru, Tuck School of Business and the Marvin Bower Fellow at Harvard. I thank you for your encouragement and guidance all throughout the journey. Despite your demanding schedule, you have been always prompt to respond to any query any time round the clock.

Girish Ganaraj, Associate Vice President, Vodafone India; Dr Kirankumar S Momaya, Professor, SJ Mehta School of Management, Indian Institute of Technology, Mumbai; Dr R K Padhy, Indian Institute of Management, Kashipur. You have reviewed the book in detail and given valuable inputs. I owe to you for your priceless support.

Dr. Vinay Sahasrabuddhe, Political Scientist, Director-Public Policy Research Center, Dr Shyamaprasad Mukherjee Nyaas and National Vice President, Bharatiya Janata Party. Your helping hand always stretched in support and guidance when I needed it the most.

Deepak Soman, former Vice President, Vodafone India. Barring me, you have spent most time with the book. You have reviewed the book, corrected it and offered suggestions. You have coaxed, pushed and inspired me when in need all throughout the journey; not to forget my unreasonable demands that you met with a smile.

Vikas Shrivastav, Life Coach who has blended Indian mystical knowledge with modern science. You have been the Melchizedek in this voyage inspiring me to rise beyond the obvious. You were just a call away whenever I was in doubt on the next step.

My family members – mother Nirupoma, wife Elora, sons Shreyam and Saptarshim, sister Cauvery. You have been constant pillars of support. You have continuously tolerated me, pampered me and provided me with whatever I needed.

Praveen Tiwari, my publisher, Bloomsbury. You have been the epitome of calmness all through my queries and unrealistic demands at frequent intervals. You have been the architect who has helped me transform the imagination into reality.

My employer, Vodafone India Ltd. and Sunil Sood, Managing Director and CEO of Vodafone India Ltd.; Ashok Ramchandran, HR Director; Laxmi Bhan, Sr. Vice President, Service Delivery; Sibaji Biswas, Executive Vice President, Supply Chain Management. It is always a challenge to write a research based book while in a full-time assignment. Your motivation and support in this journey from time to time during the research as well as later stages has immensely assisted in taking the idea to actual fruition.

V K Lakshmi. You edited the book a number of times and always stretched yourself so that the book could take better shape. Your involvement and feedback have been invaluable.

Jonathan Bill, Former Head of Innovation, Vodafone India, currently angel investor and entrepreneur; Shailesh Abhyankar, Associate Vice President, Reliance Jio. Your input during the research and testing stage was truly valuable.

All who have spared time to review and endorse the book. It has been a relentless intrusion to your busy calendars. However, you have always been welcoming and met my demands with the utmost zeal and sincerity.

Organizations where the framework was tested. Thank you for sparing your time and resources to enable me to test the practical utility of the framework.

And all others whose names I might have inadvertently missed or may not have put down in black and white. Thank you for your encouragement which has been the real motivation to pursue the journey till the end.

About the author

Gautam Kumar Borah specializes in the areas of Strategy, Innovation, Customer Operations and Business Transformation. In a career spanning over 20 years, he has worked in corporate assignments with organizations as Vodafone India, Reliance as well as in government assignments. His current assignment is with Vodafone India as part of the Customer Operations team. Gautam is a graduate in Electrical Engineering and has completed his post-graduation (Distinction) from University of Oxford specializing in Strategy and Innovation. Gautam has been a speaker at various forums in India and Overseas in his domain of expertise.

Index